Elevated
Conversations

'A book that blends practical simplicity with deep insight. Breakspear brilliantly demystifies collaboration, and provides simple, powerful tools that spark meaningful dialogue, deepen reflection, and will shift meetings from the mundane to the transformational.'
John Hattie, Laureate Professor Emeritus, Graduate School of Education, University of Melbourne

'*Elevated Conversations* is superb – it's deeply rooted in the realities of team behaviours and provides a brilliant set of tools and strategies to help teams to be more effective. More than that, it offers a whole new way of thinking about how we use our time together.'
Tom Sherrington, Director, Teaching Walkthrus

'Ask any teacher or school leader what they would like more of, and the answer is almost always the same: time. *Elevated Conversations* is a powerful reminder that impact comes not from having more time but from using it more wisely. This book delivers a fresh perspective on how we can make a difference with the moments of professional connection we have.'
Nicole West, Principal, Inglewood Primary School, Western Australia

'In the personal world of teaching with dozens of conversations a day, it can be embarrassing to think we might need help to do them better. *Elevated Conversations* provides simple and yet powerful tools with step-by-step guidance enabling us all to make our collaborative work more impactful and a real driver for sustained success.'
Courtney Howard, Principal, Cambridge Primary School, Tasmania

'There are few facilitators in the world of education who are as talented as Simon Breakspear. Fortunately for the rest of us, he has shared the tools and processes that he has developed and honed over many years in this highly practical and down-to-earth book. Anyone who wants to be able to lead meetings and manage teams better will find this book extremely useful.'
Steve Munby, Visiting Professor, University College London

'Simon Breakspear's *Elevated Conversations* puts the focus exactly where it should be in teacher professional learning, which is an achievement of productive discourse between colleagues resulting from well-planned and structured conversation protocols. This exciting new book is brim-full of many such conversation protocol gems, and I recommend it to all teachers charged with the responsibility of organising professional learning in their school.'
Tony Loughland, Associate Professor, Head of School, School of Education, UNSW

'Collaborative time is precious, but it is not always productive – this book will help you ensure you use it well. Full of tried and tested tools and strategies that will make an immediate impact, *Elevated Conversations* is a must-read for school leaders.'
Michael Rosenbrock, Co-author of *The Pruning Principle*

'*Elevated Conversations* is a timely and essential resource for educators looking to make the most of their collaborative meeting time. It offers practical tools that help teams come together with intention and clarity, strengthening meetings into meaningful opportunities for action.'
Terri Lynn Guimond, Associate Superintendent, Evergreen Catholic Separate School Division

'When educators work together with clear purpose and intent, they amplify both their individual contributions and collective impact. In *Elevated Conversations*, Simon Breakspear presents a practical approach and outlines tools designed to transform how schools collaborate. These strategies offer a game-changing pathway for teams seeking to deepen professional dialogue, align their efforts, and drive meaningful improvement in teaching and learning.'
Neil Barker, Former CEO, Bastow Institute of Educational Leadership

'Collaborative professionalism, professional learning communities, and collective responsibility all point to the central importance of collaborative time for educators. Yet practical guidance on how to make the most of that time has been limited. It is brilliant that Breakspear has produced this powerful guide to elevated conversations.'
Anthony Mackay AM, Co-Chair, Learning Creates Australia

'This book offers practical tools and strategies for schools that want to use collaboration time more purposefully. Breakspear's deep understanding of the realities schools face, combined with concrete examples from practice, makes these resources both relevant and easy to apply. A must-read for any school leader committed to lifting the quality and impact of their team's work.'
Dr Cate Challen, Senior Lecturer, Queensland University of Technology

'*Elevated Conversations* offers clear, actionable strategies to move beyond surface-level talk and into meaningful dialogue that strengthens teacher practice. This book will be a valuable tool for facilitating deeper, more purposeful conversations with staff, conversations that directly contribute to improved student outcomes.'
Leanne McGettigan, Principal, Saskatchewan, Canada

'This book doesn't ask for more time – it helps us make better use of the time we already have. I've seen firsthand how these tools can lift the quality of thinking, deepen team connection, and lead to real shifts in practice. I commend this book to every school leader who wants to elevate not just their meetings, but their impact.'
Shauna-Maree Sykes, Chief of Education, Strategy and Performance, Melbourne Archdiocese Catholic Schools

'*Elevated Conversations* is brilliant! This book, loaded with useful, practical ways to focus team conversations, is definitely a must for all school leaders who want to maximise their time and impact on students. The inclusion of examples and anecdotes is great to help people with implementation challenges. I'm looking forward to sharing this with my entire principal team.'
Leanne Peters, Assistant Superintendent, Hanover School District, Manitoba, Canada

Elevated Conversations

PRACTICAL TOOLS TO MAKE
TEACHER COLLABORATION COUNT

DR SIMON BREAKSPEAR

Published in 2025 by Amba Press, Melbourne, Australia
www.ambapress.com.au

© Simon Breakspear 2025

All rights reserved. No part of this book may be reproduced or transmitted in any form or by any means, electronic or mechanical, including photocopying, recording or by any information storage and retrieval system, without prior permission in writing from the publisher.

Cover design: Tess McCabe
Internal design: Amba Press
Developmental editor: Jaimee Vilela
Editor: Andrew Campbell

ISBN: 9781923403048 (pbk)
ISBN: 9781923403055 (ebk)

A catalogue record for this book is available from the National Library of Australia.

CONTENTS

Preface: How and Why I Wrote This Book	ix
Acknowledgments	xi
About the Author	1
Introduction: It's Time to Elevate Our Conversations	3

Part 1: The Four Ingredients of Elevated Conversations — 13

Chapter 1	Identifying Existing Team Time	17
Chapter 2	Choosing the Right Tool	21
Chapter 3	Active Facilitation	27
Chapter 4	Group Norms	35

Part 2: The Elevated Conversations Toolkit — 41

Tool 1	Empathy Square	45
Tool 2	Deeper Reasons	61
Tool 3	Outcome Heat Map	77
Tool 4	Strategy Sort	91
Tool 5	Even Better If	105
Tool 6	We Need Next	117
Tool 7	Start, Stop, Continue	129

Conclusion: Over to You	145
Appendix A: Facilitator Planning Tool	147
Appendix B: Facilitator Reflection Questions	149
References	151
Index	153

PREFACE
HOW AND WHY I WROTE THIS BOOK

You are probably working too hard when preparing for collaborative meetings and professional learning time. My team and I did too. Late nights and early mornings were often spent painstakingly preparing bespoke slides and materials. That was until we discovered the power of identifying existing time, using the right facilitation tools and engaging in active facilitation that engages teams and helps everybody productively contribute.

As educators, all of us have these blocks of 'collaborative time'. The impact of this time is determined by the quality of the conversations we have while we're in there, and unfortunately, all too often these sessions are poorly facilitated, leaving everyone disappointed and wishing they could claim their hour back. In our defence, as the ones in charge of facilitating, there's an explanation for this: the reality for many of us when pulling together these collaborative sessions is that we are time-poor. The format therefore tends to be cobbled together – it's rushed, under-prepared, and we're running on fumes, often limping along on a tired approach or agenda.

Over the years of running countless professional learning sessions and coaching team leaders, a few recurring questions began to emerge: How can we make the best use of the collaboration time we have? How can we make it so that leaders need to prepare less and yet can gain more impact? How can we broaden the sense of ownership and agency among educators responsible for running the sessions?

The conversation tools I share in this book are a simple response to these questions. They are easy to prepare, reliable to run and result in productive and tangible output every time. The best part is that the tools work for all staff, not just the super-keen volunteers. Each one provides a different way to structure team time so that it feels fresh and useful and invites whole-team participation. These tools are the rocket fuel that I hope will radically improve your collaboration time and reduce your prep workload at the same time.

I'm thrilled to share these tools with you. I hope they save you time and improve both your confidence and impact. You don't have to follow the guidance provided strictly, either – use it as a jumping-off point to adapt approaches that work for you.

My team and I are committed to enhancing the impact of school leaders' work while actively helping to reduce their cognitive and workload demands wherever we can. I hope the elevated conversations toolkit and facilitation guidance do precisely that.

In partnership for better learning,

Simon Breakspear
July 2025

ACKNOWLEDGMENTS

All of my best ideas emerge from collaborative and grounded work with generous colleagues and practitioners. *Elevated Conversations* is best understood as my attempt to codify the collective experiences, insights and adaptations of educators doing the real work in schools.

I've been fortunate to learn from a diverse group of educators and school leaders who helped me refine these tools until they became genuinely useful in practice. I'm grateful to everyone who gave their time, feedback and energy to this work.

Many of the tools in this book took shape during my work on practice improvement using the teaching sprints process (Breakspear & Jones, 2020). As we supported teams in shifting their professional conversations, we discovered how powerful simple, well-structured tools can be. Lynne Khong, Ricky Campbell-Allen, Ryan Dunn, Bronwyn Ryrie Jones and Terri Lynn Guimond were all instrumental in testing and improving the early versions of these tools. I'm grateful to Brendan Lee, who helped to sharpen the tools and contributed to many of the examples. Jeanette Breen provided a thoughtful review of the final tools.

To my friend Jaimee Vilela: thank you for being a brilliant developmental editor. You consistently help me to clarify my ideas and move forward with greater conviction.

To Alicia, Andrew and the Amba Press team, thank you for your professional and seamless support in turning a useful idea into a book ready for educators to use.

To my wife, Alice, thank you for your constant support and partnership in all things. And to my children, Sam, Eve and Josh, thank you for being my everyday inspiration to continue working on the worthy task of helping schools to keep getting better.

ABOUT THE AUTHOR

Dr Simon Breakspear is a researcher, advisor and speaker on educational leadership, policy and change. As the founder of Strategic Schools, Simon and his team develop frameworks and tools that make evidence-based ideas actionable and easy to understand. Over the last decade, his professional learning work has given him the opportunity to work with over 100,000 educators across more than ten countries.

Simon is an Adjunct Senior Lecturer in the School of Education at UNSW. He has served as an advisor to the NSW Department of Education and sits on an expert steering committee for the Australia Institute for Teaching and School Leadership (AITSL). Simon received his BPsych (Hons) from UNSW, his MSc in Comparative and International Education from the University of Oxford and his PhD in Education from the University of Cambridge. He has been a Commonwealth and Gates Scholar. Simon began his work in education as a high school teacher.

INTRODUCTION
IT'S TIME TO ELEVATE OUR CONVERSATIONS

Who among us has not walked out of a team session thinking, 'Well, that's 58 minutes I'll never get back again – what a complete waste of time'? In my day job, I'm fortunate to work alongside hundreds of school and team leaders. All of them are overloaded, stretched and pulled in multiple directions. While they are passionate about leading effective team and school-wide professional learning conversations, the reality is that they are often left underprepared and out of time when it comes to running them. All of us have been there: there are simply not enough minutes in the day, so preparation for professional conversations gets pushed to the side in favour of more urgent tasks.

Helpfully, over the years of running professional learning conversations with thousands of educators, I have developed a simple and effective approach to running high-quality professional conversations that has reduced my need to be the centre of the action. The best thing about it is that it comprises powerful, simple tools that anyone can pick up and run with. I have designed, adapted, refined and field-tested these tools over hundreds of sessions, which became my test kitchen. This book captures these codified lessons as practical professional learning recipes that any leader can pick up, modify and use. To stretch the analogy, not every meal needs to be made 'from scratch' – and the same goes for our facilitation efforts. Not every workshop or team session needs us to pore over slides and develop a wildly unique agenda – these tools are your shortcuts to a fruitful session every time.

This book will not tell you precisely what to do in your collaborative time, but it will surface powerful ways of working and adaptable processes that team leaders can use to elevate the quality of their time together. In short, it will teach you how to run what I like to call 'elevated conversations'. The results of such conversations should be to:

- **Elevate discussion** – go from talking in circles to using structured frameworks
- **Elevate thinking** – stimulate fresh ideas and approaches, and generate new insights
- **Elevate connections** – feel a sense of the collective
- **Elevate practice** – take new action and reframe the problems to be solved
- **Elevate energy** – rejuvenate and refresh the team.

The goal is for our teams to leave a session saying to themselves in surprise, 'Wow, I really enjoyed that – it's given me a lot to think about and it feels like we actually made some progress together'.

Making better use of the time we already have

Having better conversations is about making our existing collaborative meeting times far more meaningful and impactful. While we would all love to secure additional collaborative time together, the low-hanging fruit is clearly for us to start making better use of the time that we already have. If our existing 'together time' isn't moving things forward, extra time won't necessarily help!

> If our existing "together time" isn't moving things forward, extra time won't necessarily help!

The unfortunate reality is that effective collaboration time doesn't just emerge naturally by getting people together. We can get educators together in the same place but still fail to talk about the most valuable things in productive ways. I call this being stuck 'below the line' in weary talk.

Elevated Conversations

Weary Talk

Weary talk in a collaborative meeting can look like this:

- Some people are distracted by their laptop, phone or tablet. They glance up now and again, but keep tapping away at their emails.
- Somebody thinks they know it all and dominates the discussion. When you think they've finally finished, they return to 'holding the floor' after your next question prompt.
- You keep running out of time before getting to the heart of the problem to be solved.
- Certain people get into turf wars and engage in the same old disagreements.
- A single person monopolises the entire time to download and debrief about a recent tricky interaction with a student or parent.
- Some people do not contribute anything, even after you directly prompt and ask them for input.

Which of these scenarios stand out as regular points of frustration in your own collaborative time?

I don't place judgment on any individuals here. The reality is, it is difficult for all of us to switch from teaching mode to collaboration mode. We are often still unpacking and making sense of a recent student interaction, or already beginning to think about a commitment we will head to straight after the session. At other times, we feel ourselves rapidly crashing and suddenly realise mid-session how drained we are.

We can all empathise with the behaviour of staff – and ourselves – caused by overwhelm and overload. We can understand why our team's minds might be more focused on other things rather than being actively engaged. Often, we ask people to switch from teacher mode to collaboration mode just moments after stepping out of the classroom and pulling a chair up around a team meeting. It's a leap for any of us.

> … we ask people to switch from teacher mode to collaboration mode just moments after stepping out of the classroom.

Enabling better professional conversations

As the leaders tasked with facilitating these conversations, it's our responsibility to make sure our sessions are run well, stay above the line and avoid dropping off into weary talk. We need to intentionally plan for how best to engage teachers in robust discussions about their practice and playing their role in broader school improvement.

How do we get there? This book provides you with seven practical conversation tools to reset and elevate your existing team sessions. The approaches we share have been field-tested with hundreds of teacher teams around the world and aim to help you enhance the relevance and impact of your collaborative time together and get more engagement from your colleagues. The best news is that leveraging these tools will also significantly reduce your workload – and mental load – as a leader, making it easy to facilitate like a pro with proven 'done for you' templates and steps.

The elevated conversations toolkit

This book is a curated compilation of tools and approaches that have been tested, adapted and refined in real schools. While not all of the ideas are new, they've been selected because they consistently work, especially in the hands of busy leaders navigating complex team environments.

The table below outlines each of the conversational tools and summarises their purpose. You might think of this collection as a practical recipe book. It offers a set of options that you can draw on, depending on the challenge, the context and the composition of the group. These tools aren't designed to solve every interpersonal group challenge, but they will help you structure time more effectively and guide teams toward more effective conversations and clearer outcomes.

Each tool can be used independently. Or they can be brought together in sequence to create a purposeful flow of thinking, reflection and decision-making over a given session, term or year. Throughout the book, we will help you understand, adapt and apply them to your context.

#	Tool	Purpose
1	Empathy Square	Uncover deep insights about learners' experiences and needs
2	Deeper Reasons	Explore why students might be struggling to make progress
3	Outcome Heat Map	Visualise the most important and hard-to-teach learning outcomes to focus on
4	Strategy Sort	Review a range of solutions based on their potential impact versus the effort required
5	Even Better If	Gain fast, helpful peer feedback to improve the quality of our work
6	We Need Next	Identify professional growth aspirations and actions
7	Start, Stop, Continue	Work out what we need to do in order to maximise our effectiveness

How to use the tools in this book

All of the tools we will use to elevate our conversations serve distinct purposes. They help to facilitate dynamic and inclusive conversations that solve problems and generate actionable ways forward. It's really about moving away from passive exchanges and prioritising active co-construction. Throughout the book, we outline clear steps and provide facilitator tips for making it happen with your teams.

Each tool has a template linked to it. These templates don't just provide the direction for the conversation and thinking, but allow for a third focus point, and therefore an opportunity for three-point communication. This is important because in a typical conversation, you'll have two people talking face-to-face, in two-point communication. The beauty of having a 'third point' is that it is something that the facilitator and participants can focus on together – the visual resource helps the session become 'us against the problem' rather than 'me against you' when certain discussions have the potential to become emotionally charged (Grinder, 1997). The template moves the visual focus away from the participants and toward the reflections that have been documented.

In general, a third point also makes for a more objective and collaborative experience. It allows each person to participate and have an opportunity to articulate their thoughts. Additionally, engaging in writing rather than solely discussing ideas verbally, compels participants to carefully consider their thoughts before expressing them. It also brings underlying assumptions and differences of opinion out into the open.

The template can simply be downloaded and printed out, but often it will be better to go bigger! As we want it to be a shared template, it needs to be visible to all participants. This might mean drawing the template up on a whiteboard or using butcher's paper. Sticky notes are also a great way for teachers to generate individual ideas that can be easily moved around and combined into a collective output.

Key design features of the elevated conversations toolkit

These conversational tools feature many strengths for improving conversations with busy professionals:

- **Time-bound** – they can be run during 15–50-minute pockets of collaborative time.
- **Clear purpose** – different tools help teams to move through distinctive stages of thinking and sharing to achieve a desired purpose.
- **Structured process** – tools provide a structured template to support educator teams in addressing common challenges and deepening important conversations.
- **Inclusive** – they help to ensure that progress is made and everyone's voice is heard, even when group members are tired and feeling overloaded.
- **Third-point conversations** – by capturing thinking in a shared visual template, educators can make their thinking about practice explicit and open it up to the input of their colleagues.
- **Tangible output** – the summary template and responses to key questions provide a shared outcome with insights and decisions that can shape future action.
- **Broader ownership** – systems and processes also alleviate the need to rely on the expertise of individuals and move into a space of empowering the team. Because of the simple structures and processes, the tools can be facilitated by any team member, not just the 'official' leader.

How to use this book

The book has two parts.

In Part 1, we outline and unpack the four ingredients for elevated conversations. In Part 2, we provide a detailed overview of the elevated conversations toolkit, including the purpose, template, steps and facilitation guidance you'll need to bring the tools to life.

These tools will give you a structured approach to facilitating more elevated conversations together. We hope you can use this book as a practical facilitator playbook. It should look well used by the end of the year, with hand-written notes, highlights and dog-eared pages throughout. Keep it on hand for most weeks of the term.

Let's get into it.

> More information about elevated conversations and links to online resources throughout the book can be found at
> **https://elevatedconversations.com.au**

> The discipline of team learning starts with "dialogue", the capacity of members of a team to suspend assumptions and enter into a genuine "thinking together".
>
> – *Peter Senge (2006, p. 10)*

> By participating in thoughtful conversations about practice, teachers acquire valuable habits of mind that enable them to pursue such thinking on their own, without the scaffolding provided by the particular conversation.
>
> – *Charlotte Danielson (2012, p. 21)*

> Discovering you were wrong doesn't have to threaten your intelligence or bruise your ego. It can be a sign that you've learned something. Few of us enjoy *being* wrong. Finding joy in *having been wrong* is a step towards keeping an open mind.
>
> – *Adam Grant (2021, p. 5)*

> Facilitation is creating conditions for a group to learn from one another, make progress on goals, and accomplish a task. Facilitation is a skill that can be taught and practised.
>
> – *Emily Boudreau (2019)*

PART 1

The Four Ingredients of Elevated Conversations

Part 1 provides an overview of the four core ingredients required for developing an elevated conversation moment. These four ingredients are the foundation of every successful team session – they help ensure the time you spend together is focused, practical and energising.

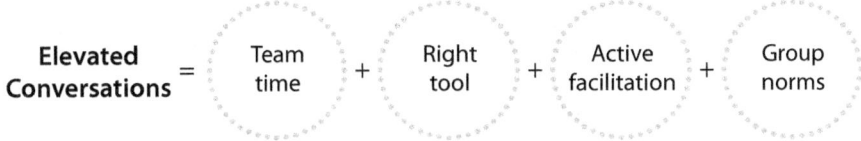

Chapter 1 focuses on the first ingredient: team time. It is about identifying the existing collaborative pockets of time that are available. Once you identify the collaborative time that you already have, you can go about trying to enhance the impact from this time. The key question here is: What currently available pockets of collaborative time can you better leverage?

Chapter 2 unpacks the right tool. This is about knowing your team's challenges and selecting the right conversation tool(s) for the desired outcome. The key question here is: Which tool or combination of tools will help you engage in the right professional conversation for this challenge?

Chapter 3 explores how to run the tool well with your team through active facilitation. While you don't need to be a rock-star trainer, there are some simple, crucial steps that will help you to activate the tool properly with your team. The goal here is to lead in a way that activates the room – the tool is the match, but you need to light it in order to create the desired effect. The tool will not work unless you do. The key question here is: What role do you need to play in order to effectively activate this tool with your team so that you have an engaged, fruitful session?

Chapter 4 examines the significance of robust group norms. Even with a well-chosen tool and confident facilitation, the success of a session often hinges on how people behave in the room. This chapter outlines three foundational norms that support productive team dialogue: stick to what matters, make room for new thinking, and invite healthy challenge. The key question here is: What shared ways of working will help your team stay focused, open and constructive during collaboration?

CHAPTER 1
IDENTIFYING EXISTING TEAM TIME

The key question here is: What currently available pockets of collaborative time can you better leverage?

I often hear school leaders say, 'We don't have any spare time,' or 'There's no space left in the calendar.' However, in the next breath, they describe weekly team meetings, stage planning sessions, or organise collaborative blocks that regularly underdeliver.

This is the real opportunity. Most schools will not be able to find more time: they need to make the most of the time they already have.

The way teams use their collaborative time sends a strong cultural signal. Allowing unstructured or unclear sessions suggests that our shared time isn't valued. However, when time is used effectively, with clarity, focus and shared responsibility, it strengthens team culture and fosters professional momentum.

As I outlined in the introduction, when time is poorly used, it often drifts into what I call 'weary talk' – sessions that fill the calendar but drain energy. Updates drag on, dominant voices take over, and the most important work is deferred. These low-yield conversations are easy to fall into, especially when preparation time is short or facilitation feels hard to manage.

The first step in breaking this pattern is to identify the blocks of time we already have. Rather than adding more collaboration time, the approach I advocate for is about being more intentional with the time that already exists. It's about reshaping how we meet so that thinking improves, decisions get made and teams feel a sense of progress.

Identifying promising opportunities

There's no one 'right' moment for collaboration. Every school has a different rhythm, but nearly all have existing opportunities that can be used more effectively.

Common examples include:

- Small group discussions
- Team/grade/stage/faculty meetings
- Curriculum planning time
- Data analysis sessions
- Professional learning communities (PLCs) or professional learning teams (PLTs)
- Instructional or peer coaching
- New staff mentoring sessions
- Development and goal-setting conversations
- Full-school professional learning sessions
- Staff development days
- Case management meetings about key students.

The tools in this book can be used with any group size. For large groups, such as full-staff sessions, it's best to break into smaller teams to ensure everyone has space to contribute. Each group can work through the same tool, with a facilitator guiding the process and a lead facilitator coordinating across the room.

Auditing your existing collaborative time

Once you've identified the blocks, the next step is to understand how they're currently working. A practical way to do this is to audit each block and assess how well it's being used.

For each one, consider:

- Who attends?
- How often does it occur?
- What is the total time available across a term?
- What's the current focus or format?
- How effective is it now? Use stars or descriptors such as low/medium/high.
- What is its potential to be elevated through better tools?

Table 1: Audit table template

Collaboration block / frequency	Who attends?	Total time per term	Current focus	Current effectiveness
Team meetings *Weekly*	Grade or faculty teachers	10 × 60 mins = 10 hrs	Curriculum planning and data review	★★★★☆
Instructional coaching *Twice a term*	Instructional coach + beginning teachers	2 × 90 mins = 3 hrs	Mixed focus	★★★☆☆
Professional learning teams *Monthly*	Cross-grade teams	3 × 60 mins = 3 hrs	Practice improvement on formative assessment	★★☆☆☆
Staff PD days *Once per term*	Whole staff	1 × 5 hrs = 5 hrs	Information updates Research to inform practice	★☆☆☆☆

Once you've mapped your collaboration time, look for gaps between the total time available and the value it currently delivers. You might find that a large portion of staff time is already scheduled, but very little of it leads to genuine shared thinking or forward movement. Choose one or two blocks that feel underleveraged and start there. You don't need a full redesign, just better use of a few of your current blocks.

The goal is not to find additional time. It's to make smarter use of what's already built into the week. By identifying when and where collaborative sessions already happen, and applying just enough structure to guide the conversation, schools can dramatically improve what those sessions deliver.

What part of your team's existing meeting time could be restructured to create more value?

> **SUMMARY OF CHAPTER 1: IDENTIFYING EXISTING TEAM TIME**
>
> - Most schools will not be able to gain more collaboration time, so the opportunity lies in using what's already in the calendar more effectively.
>
> - Start by identifying the regular blocks of time where teams already meet.
>
> - Map who attends, how often they meet and what that time is currently used for.
>
> - Use the audit process to assess how effective each block is and where there's room to improve.
>
> - Choose one or two opportunities to redesign first. Start small, and build from there.

CHAPTER 2
CHOOSING THE RIGHT TOOL

The key question here is: Which tool or combination of tools will help you engage in the right professional conversation for this challenge?

Once you've identified when collaboration time is available, the next challenge is knowing how to use it. Many leaders find themselves asking, 'I know we need to talk about this, but how should we structure the conversation?'

Choosing the right tool begins with clarity about what kind of conversation your team needs right now. Are you trying to surface insights? Prioritise? Solve a persistent problem? Refine something that's already in motion?

This is where the elevated conversations toolkit becomes a practical asset. It doesn't give you a rigid script. It gives you structure and a set of flexible formats to guide purposeful thinking and shared decision-making.

Think of the tools as your coffee pods. They're quick to prepare, reliably effective and easy to run. Like different pods, each tool has its own flavour and function, designed for a particular kind of conversation. You don't need to invent a session from scratch. You just need to select the right option for the purpose and then use your own facilitation skills to bring out the flavour.

As outlined in Table 2, each conversation tool has a specific purpose and driving question.

Table 2: Conversation tools

#	Name / description	Purpose	Key question
1	**Empathy Square** *Attunement to others*	Uncover deep insights about learners' experiences and needs	How can we understand this experience from the stance of a learner?
2	**Deeper Reasons** *Problem analysis and reframings*	Explore why students might be struggling to make progress	What's the core challenge we need to make progress on?
3	**Outcome Heat Map** *Prioritising effort*	Visualise the most important and hard-to-teach learning outcomes to focus on	Which essential outcomes will be hardest to teach?
4	**Strategy Sort** *Solution-finding*	Review a range of solutions based on their potential impact versus effort required	What is a workable and realistic solution?
5	**Even Better If** *Refining and enhancing*	Gain fast, helpful peer feedback to improve the quality of our work	How can we refine and improve our work and ways of working?
6	**We Need Next** *Professional growth and development*	Identify professional learning aspirations and actions	How can we keep growing as professionals?
7	**Start, Stop, Continue** *Workflow change*	Work out what we need to do in order to maximise team effectiveness	What's helping, what's hindering, and what needs to evolve?

To download online resources for these tools, go to

https://elevatedconversations.com.au

Matching the tool to the moment

As you scan the table opposite, think about recent collaborative sessions. What outcome were you hoping for? Where did the conversation stall? When did people seem energised? Which of the tools might have helped?

Now you can start to think about future sessions. The goal is to generate lots of potential use cases for when a certain tool might be useful. Ask yourself: when might be a particularly useful time or context for each one, throughout the rhythm of the month, term or year?

For example, an instructional coach may see an opportunity to use the Empathy Square tool to help teachers work out why persistent problems in their classroom might be occurring. Or a school leader might use the We Need Next tool at the end of a meeting about upcoming curriculum change to prioritise the next steps for professional learning.

The tools we will use to elevate our conversations serve distinct purposes. They help to facilitate dynamic and inclusive conversations that solve problems and generate actionable ways forward. It's really about moving away from passive exchanges and prioritising active engagement.

Which tools and in what order?

The tools can be used in a number of ways – individually or sequenced in groups. Some of them can help us prioritise what we need to focus on (Outcome Heat Map and Strategy Sort); others can be used to analyse situations (Empathy Square and Deeper Reasons); and some can help us assess the current state (We Need Next, Even Better If and Start, Stop, Continue).

Sometimes a single tool is all you need. Other times, combining two tools in sequence can help a team go deeper or move from insight to action. For example:

- You might use the Even Better If tool to gain feedback on some work and then pair it up with the We Need Next tool to decide the next steps for professional development to implement it effectively.

- The Outcome Heat Map tool might tell you that there is a common area that is 'Essential to learn' and 'Harder to teach'. Going through the Strategy Sort tool could then help decide what strategies could be used to teach that identified priority outcome.
- Using the Empathy Square tool might have you wanting more answers for why you have a particular problem, in which case you might follow up by using the Deeper Reasons tool to examine why those patterns exist in the first place.

In most cases you can plan these combinations of tools in advance. At other times, the need will emerge in the moment, and you can lead the team toward whatever feels most relevant, adapting as needed.

Look for natural entry points

The goal is to decide which conversation tool is relevant – when and with whom. There's no need to wait for the 'perfect' session. Look for moments when you can build a tool into the collaborative work you're already doing. For example, when:

- Discussing a focus area your team has been exploring
- Unpacking mandated curriculum or policy changes
- Reflecting on a program or strategy that's just been implemented
- Fine-tuning plans before the start of a new unit, cycle or term
- Looking at data
- Coming to the end of a professional learning cycle.

The table opposite shows how typical collaboration moments can be lifted with the right tool.

Table 3: Lifting collaboration moments

Move from this	To this
Asking, 'Does anyone have any students of concern?'	Empathy Square
Someone presenting the latest assessment results	Deeper Reasons
Just watching a video describing the impending curriculum changes	Outcome Heat Map
School leaders telling teachers what they need to change in their classroom practice	Strategy Sort
Teachers individually refining units of work	Even Better If
Closing off a cycle of professional learning with an abrupt stop point	We Need Next
Continuing with ineffective meeting processes because that's the way it's always been done	Start, Stop, Continue

SUMMARY OF CHAPTER 2: CHOOSING THE RIGHT TOOL

- Each tool has a distinct purpose – choose the one that best fits the current challenge.
- Use prompts and recent experience to guide your selection.
- Tools can be combined to help teams move through interconnected modes of thinking and discussion.
- When in doubt, keep it simple. One well-matched tool, used well, is enough to shift the conversation.

CHAPTER 3
ACTIVE FACILITATION

> The tool will not work unless you do.
> The key question here is: What role do you need to play in order to effectively activate this tool with your team so that you have an engaged, fruitful session?

You don't need to be a master facilitator to lead a great collaborative session. But you do need to be deliberate. Even simple tools only work when someone takes responsibility for setting the tone, guiding the process and keeping things moving.

That's your role.

Active facilitation is about creating the conditions for people to think well together. It's not about delivering content or performing for the group. It's about leading a session with purpose, clarity and just enough structure to help people stay focused and engaged.

As outlined in Table 4, the most effective facilitators do three things: they set things up well, they run the session with confidence and care, and they close in motion, so the work continues after the conversation ends. Appendix A provides a session planner that can help you structure your thinking ahead of a team gathering using a tool.

Table 4: The key roles for active facilitation

#	Phase	Key actions
1	Set it up	Clarify the purpose. Prepare the space. Anticipate where the conversation might get stuck. Rehearse the flow.
2	Run the session	Guide, prompt and pace the discussion. Follow the structure of the tool. Keep people focused and engaged.
3	Close in motion	Summarise progress. Capture the thinking so it can be carried forward. Name the next steps.

1. Set it up

Before you walk into the room, spend 5–10 minutes visualising how the session will run. Ask yourself:

- What's the purpose of this session?
- What do I want people to walk away with?
- Where will the conversation likely get stuck?

The goal isn't to have a perfect plan: it's to feel confident enough to guide the session calmly and clearly.

Make the purpose clear from the start. Don't assume everyone knows why you're meeting. Even one sentence is enough: 'We're here to unpack why progress has stalled in this unit and make a plan to reset. We are going to use the Start, Stop, Continue tool to help structure our discussion.' This helps people shift gears and engage more deeply.

Prepare the space. Will you use A3 templates or work on a whiteboard? Will people work in pairs or small groups? What's the energy in the room likely to be, and how might you need to shift it? If it's been a long day, open with a moment of humour, movement or reflection to reset the tone.

Have prompts or slides ready if needed. You don't need a deck. A printed question or two can be enough to keep things on track.

2. Run the session

Facilitation is not the same as presenting. You are not there to talk; rather you are there to guide, listen, redirect and invite.

Here are some core practices that will help:

- **Set the expectations early** – Remind the group that this is a working session, not a sit-and-get. Ask everyone to be fully present and contribute in some form.
- **Use energy intentionally** – Pay attention to the tempo of the session. When the room feels flat, shift to pair discussion. When energy is high but scattered, bring people back to the central task.
- **Stay with the process** – Don't let the group drift into general discussion too early. Follow the steps of the tool you're using and be ready to say, 'Let's hold that for the next step.'
- **Draw everyone in** – Use prompts like 'What's coming to mind for you?' 'I'd be interested to hear your thoughts on this.' 'What else might we be missing here? or 'How does this align with your perspective?' to gently invite quieter voices into the conversation. Use a Reflect–Discuss–Share routine to give everyone time to form their thinking individually, explore it in pairs or trios, and then bring their insights to the whole group.
- **Avoid dominating the thinking** – Don't solve the problem yourself. Resist the urge to fix or explain too soon. Let the group sit with ambiguity. See if insights emerge naturally.
- **Capture as you go** – Assign someone to write on the board or template. Make ideas visible so others can respond to what's been said, not just what's remembered.

3. Close in motion

Facilitation doesn't stop when the timer runs out. Great sessions don't end with 'Thanks, everyone.' They end with clear takeaways, next steps and shared momentum.

Use these final minutes to:

- **Name what was achieved** – 'We've identified three key causes and prioritised next actions.'
- **Decide what happens next** – 'We'll regroup in two weeks to see how those adjustments went.'
- **Document the work** – Take a photo of the board or template and share it with the group via email or a Microsoft Teams thread.
- **Acknowledge the contribution** – 'Thanks for leaning into this – we got further than expected.'

It's better to leave with one clear decision about next steps than five unfinished ideas.

> ### Common facilitation traps
>
> Even experienced leaders can fall into these unhelpful patterns:
>
> - **Over-talking** – filling every silence rather than giving space to think
> - **Over-explaining** – adding too much context or justification at the start
> - **Jumping steps** – rushing into open discussion before the tool has done its work
> - **Ignoring energy** – pushing through when the group needs a reset
> - **Not capturing the thinking** – letting great ideas vanish because no one wrote them down.
>
> Spotting these patterns, then debriefing with a colleague, is one of the quickest ways to sharpen your facilitation.

Improving over time

Each tool has been carefully structured based on field-testing with hundreds of school teams. Follow the steps as outlined and you'll have everything you need for a productive session that flows smoothly. But facilitation is not a fixed recipe. Once you're confident with the process, there's room to adapt, rework and make it your own. The tools are designed to be flexible, so you can respond to the needs of your team, your context and the moment you're in.

Facilitation is a practice. You'll improve each time you lead. Some sessions will feel clunky or awkward. Don't worry, that's normal. What matters most is showing up with intention, keeping the work focused and creating space for others to contribute and come to their own insights and conclusions. Appendix B offers some key reflection questions that you can use to learn from experience and improve over time.

You don't need to be perfect. Just be present, prepared and willing to guide the room.

As your team becomes more familiar with the tools, look for opportunities to share the facilitation role. You don't have to lead every session; part of your job is to build others' confidence and create a culture where facilitation is a shared responsibility.

Mastering facilitation: top tips

1. How to set up the task and explain what you are going to do and why

Facilitators often say the hardest part is the first 90 seconds – getting people into the right mindset and giving just enough context without over-explaining. The key is to be clear on *why* the tool matters for this moment in time. Link it to something real ('We've all been noticing X, and this tool helps us explore Y'). Avoid jumping straight into the steps; begin with the purpose and the shared challenge the group is about to tackle. A confident, concise introduction sets the tone and saves you from having to backtrack or clarify later.

2. When you might ask the group to just read the tool outline so they know what it is all about

Sometimes the simplest move is to let the tool speak for itself – especially if the team is already familiar with the format. If energy is low or time is tight, invite them to read the short description silently first, then prompt with: 'How might this help us move our thinking forward?' or 'What step in the tool is likely to bring the most value to our collective thinking?' This builds shared understanding without you having to do all the talking. It also empowers teams to eventually run tools themselves.

3. Supporting individual thinking before group discussion

It's tempting to jump straight into discussion, but if people haven't had time to think, only the quickest (or loudest) voices will be heard. Build in 2–4 minutes of solo reflection at the start: sticky notes, jotting on the template, or just quiet time with a prompt. You'll get higher-quality contributions, and people are more likely to speak if they've already clarified their own thinking first and written it down.

4. Working out when to use pairs

Pairs are your facilitation secret weapon. Use them when energy drops, when you want to warm people up before a bigger share-out, or when a topic might be vulnerable. Pairs are especially helpful after individual thinking, as people can test out their ideas in a low-pressure space before bringing them to the group. They're also great for unlocking quieter voices who might not jump into a whole-group discussion.

5. Moving to capture the group's thinking

One of the biggest risks is staying in conversation mode too long and not externalising the thinking. Prompt regularly: 'Let's write that down' or 'Can someone capture that on a sticky note?' or 'What should we add to the template?' The shared visual capture becomes the group's memory, and helps turn talk into insight. You can even nominate a scribe to help keep this flowing as you facilitate.

6. Dealing with disagreement or different opinions

Disagreement is healthy, but it can feel risky in a group. Use your facilitator voice to normalise it: 'Great, we've got different views here. That's where the good stuff emerges.' Pause and prompt deeper thinking: 'Can you tell us a bit more about what makes you suggest that?' 'Can you flesh it out a little more for us?' 'What's behind your view?' 'Can you take us a little deeper about how you came to that answer?' Remind the group that we're not aiming for immediate consensus – we're aiming for clarity, insight and better collective decisions. Structure helps here too – the steps in the tools keep the debate productive and anchored.

7. Using the question prompts in the tool description or the template

Don't feel pressure to use *every* question. Skim the prompts before the session and choose the ones that best match your group's focus. Keep a few handy as 'lifters' if the conversation stalls or stays too surface-level. Good prompts bring the room into sharper focus and help people move from general talk to specific insight.

8. How to get people to a decision/action point

Great conversations still need a landing. As energy starts to dip, gently move the group toward action: 'How can we best synthesise our collective position, including remaining points of disagreement?' 'What do we want to take forward from this?' 'What would a good next step look like here?' Even if you don't fully finish the tool, aim to leave with a clear takeaway or commitment. Capture it visibly and confirm who's doing what, and by when.

9. Capturing the work done: taking a photo/documenting it

The work won't stick if it disappears. At the end of a session, pause for one minute to document – take a photo of the template, transcribe sticky notes, or upload to a shared folder or doc. If it's physical, snap it before you pack up. Nominate someone to 'own' the capture if you're facilitating. That record is gold for collectively building on thinking over time, and shows the team that their thinking matters.

SUMMARY OF CHAPTER 3: ACTIVE FACILITATION

- Facilitation is about guiding purposeful conversations, not presenting or managing.
- Strong facilitators focus on creating the right conditions for others to think, contribute and make progress.
- Effective sessions follow three key phases:
  1. **Set it up** – clarify purpose, prepare the space, plan the flow
  2. **Run the session** – hold the structure, draw in all voices, manage energy
  3. **Close in motion** – capture outcomes, confirm next steps, and document the work.

CHAPTER 4
GROUP NORMS

The key question here is: What shared ways of working will help your team stay focused, open and constructive during collaboration?

Even with a great tool and a confident facilitator, a session can still fall flat. Sometimes, it's not the process or the preparation, but rather the team dynamics in the room.

That's where group norms come in.

Shared norms are the behavioural expectations that help teams think clearly together, stay focused and make progress. When they're in place, conversations flow. When they're absent, sessions can stall in vague talk, safe agreement or silence. Norms are the social scaffolding that allows deeper work to happen.

The mistake many teams make is assuming that norms will emerge on their own. But productive collaboration doesn't just happen. It needs to be explicitly named, modelled and reinforced.

Norms are not rules. They're habits of interaction: the behaviours we expect from one another when we work together. They do three things:

1. **Create safety** – by clarifying expectations for participation
2. **Increase quality** – by shaping how people respond to ideas and feedback

3. **Build consistency** – by giving sessions a familiar rhythm, no matter who is facilitating.

You don't need ten. You just need a few clear expectations that help everyone show up well and stay in the work. Let's start with three foundational norms.

As outlined in Table 5, these three norms can help teams think clearly together, stay focused and make meaningful progress.

Table 5: Three foundational norms

#	Norm	What it means	Why it helps
1	Stick to what matters	Stay focused on the purpose of the session and avoid unproductive tangents.	Keeps the team grounded in the work and makes the most of limited time.
2	Make room for new thinking	Invite fresh ideas and different perspectives. Pause the familiar.	Prevents 'groupthink' and encourages creativity and deeper insight.
3	Invite healthy challenge	Encourage respectful disagreement to sharpen thinking and improve decisions.	Builds trust and improves the quality of collective decisions.

Three foundational norms

The three foundational norms are simple enough to be remembered, but powerful enough to shape the quality of your team's collaboration. They reflect the natural arc of a great conversation, beginning with focus, opening up to new thinking, and welcoming productive challenge.

Each norm is practical. Each one makes a difference. Together, they support the kinds of conversations that lead to clarity, progress and shared ownership.

1. Stick to what matters

When conversations drift, energy drops. This norm helps teams stay focused on the core purpose of the session and avoid getting sidetracked by tangents, war stories or unrelated issues. It's not about rigid control; it's about staying focused on what the session is for.

You can reinforce this norm by:

- Naming the purpose clearly at the start
- Using a visible question or task to anchor the group
- Asking participants to use pens and Post-it notes to capture thinking in real time
- Having a 'carpark' where unrelated ideas, problems or questions can be logged if they come up during the session.

It also connects to how we record and reflect on what we're doing. Writing things down on a board, template or shared screen helps hold attention and reduce distraction. It also makes it easier to return to the thinking later.

2. Make room for new thinking

Busy teams often default to a predictable, ingrained groove of thinking, circling around the same ideas, perspectives and voices. This norm is about opening the door to curiosity. It encourages the team to explore, extend and remain open to different ways of viewing the problem.

You can reinforce this norm by:

- Asking: 'What haven't we considered yet?'
- Creating individual thinking time before paired or group discussion
- Using prompts like: 'What's another way to look at this?' or 'Who sees it differently?'
- Encouraging people to build on each other's thinking instead of holding tight to their own view.

This is also where collaborative construction happens. When we say 'Yes, and...' instead of 'Yes, but...', we move from parallel thinking to shared thinking.

3. Invite healthy challenge

Great teams challenge each other, not to score points, but to sharpen the work. This norm helps make that challenge feel safe and expected. It encourages people to speak up when something doesn't sit right, and to listen carefully when someone sees it differently.

You can reinforce this norm by:

- Normalising pushback: 'Disagreement is welcome if it helps us think'
- Encouraging dissent: 'Is anyone seeing it another way?'
- Pausing to explore tension or uncertainty instead of rushing through it
- Modelling what respectful challenge sounds like.

This is how a team moves beyond politeness and into deeper trust. It's not always comfortable, but it's necessary if we want our conversations to lead somewhere useful.

Making the norms yours

You don't need to start from scratch. Use the three core norms in this chapter as a starting point. Then, co-develop what they look like in practice with your team.

A simple process:

1. **Introduce the norms** – Share the three norms with your team and explain how they can strengthen your collaboration. Write each up in a table on a whiteboard or large sheet of butcher's paper.
2. **Ask: 'What could this look like for us?'** – For each norm, invite people to give practical examples of what this could look like for your team in practice. Focus on describing what team members would say or do. Capture the language they use on your shared board or paper.

3. **Refine and re-language** – If a team wants to adjust the wording or add one or two extra norms, let them. What matters most is that the language feels natural, useful and owned.
4. **Make them visible and revisitable** – Write your shared version up and bring it into future sessions. Revisit and refine them over time. Norms can be laminated, but even more importantly, they need to be enacted.

This norm-setting process takes about 30 minutes and works well after completing a few tool sessions.

Norming your group

Imagine a team sitting down to use one of the conversation tools – let's say Strategy Sort – to work through a shared challenge. The facilitator opens the session, but things soon start to drift. The group gets caught up in debriefing a tricky student situation. A couple of people dive into an energised back-and-forth, while others go quiet and work on unrelated tasks on their laptops. The conversation slips into familiar grooves: ideas they've all heard before, circling without fresh insight or progress. No one's doing anything wrong, but the session starts to feel like just another meeting.

Now imagine the same team, but this time they're working with shared group norms.

Partway through, someone says, 'Let's stick to what matters – we're here to land on a few strategies worth trialling.' The team resets. A little later, someone else asks, 'What haven't we considered yet?' and a new insight surfaces from a team member who hasn't shared anything yet. Near the end, a team member gently challenges a popular idea – and instead of brushing past it, the group leans in and takes time to review their assumptions. The norms aren't just printed out; they're being put into action.

It's not flawless. But it's focused, constructive and energising. That's what strong collaborative norms make possible.

You don't need a long list of behaviours or a glossy poster. You just need a few shared ways of working that you return to over time. Norms are built through repetition. They grow stronger each time a group member names them or reinforces them explicitly.

The more your team sees these norms in action, the more they'll become part of how you meet and how you work together beyond the meeting itself. These small shifts in behaviour add up. Over time, norms evolve from helpful reminders into part of your team's professional identity. When these norms are embedded in how your team works, the tools in Part 2 become even more powerful. Shared ways of working provide the foundation for deeper dialogue and more productive collaboration.

SUMMARY OF CHAPTER 4: BUILDING STRONG COLLABORATIVE NORMS

- Even with a strong tool and facilitator, the success of a session depends on how people engage in the room.
- Norms are shared habits that help teams focus, think well together and make progress.
- They don't emerge on their own, but rather they need to be explicitly named, modelled and reinforced.
- Three foundational norms can lift the quality of any collaborative session:
    1. **Stick to what matters** – stay focused on the task and avoid drifting into distraction.
    2. **Make room for new thinking** – pause the familiar and explore different perspectives.
    3. **Invite healthy challenge** – welcome disagreement that sharpens the work and deepens shared thinking.

PART 2

The Elevated Conversations Toolkit

In Part 2, I provide comprehensive guidance on how to understand and run each of the tools with teams.

I hope this toolkit will radically improve your collaboration time and reduce your workload. You don't have to follow the guidance provided strictly, either – use it as a jumping-off point and adapt approaches that work for you.

Each tool has the following components:

- Why you should use it: An overview of why the facilitator might choose a particular tool.
- What the facilitator needs to prepare: Are there any resources the facilitator needs to prepare or data that needs to be collected?
- A series of steps to follow: What the facilitator and participants have to do and think about throughout the process.
- Tips and insights that I've learned in the field.

Adapt the process to your context

A clear process ensures that everyone can contribute and enables collaborative thinking and peer challenge in a safe environment. Each tool has a series of steps to follow – check these beforehand and consider how the tool will work best in your context. Each tool is flexible; it's not intended to be a rigid process to follow, but rather has been designed for facilitators to adapt for what works best for the team. If no-one likes 'spicy food', leave the 'chilli' out.

In the early period of learning the materials, however, we recommend that you follow the tool exactly as it is set out. We have intentionally laid out each step and field-tested it with thousands of educators. So, you might benefit from following the steps as they are, and then once you have got the hang of it, modify it based on the group's needs or your own facilitation style.

Start small

The first time you use an elevated conversations tool, it will be like cooking a recipe for the first time. You will miss a step, it will feel clunky, and you will have to go back to the shop because you forgot the saffron! The trick is to cook it a second time, because then you'll understand what you need to prepare, how long things will take and what it should look like. By the third time, you will be in a natural rhythm and groove.

> To download online resources for these tools, go to
> https://elevatedconversations.com.au

TOOL 1
EMPATHY SQUARE

Uncover deep insights about learners' experiences and needs

The Empathy Square is a focused exercise to help you put yourself into someone else's shoes – for example, those of a student or group of students – in order to better understand how to solve a challenge and improve their outcomes.

Use this tool to:

- help you to get to know your students better and tune in to their experiences of learning
- gain a greater understanding of why specific students may not be making the desired progress in a specific area
- get into the 'heads and hearts' of your students and think about how their cognitive and emotional state might be affecting how they learn
- consider the interconnections between emotion, motivation and cognition.

Empathy Square

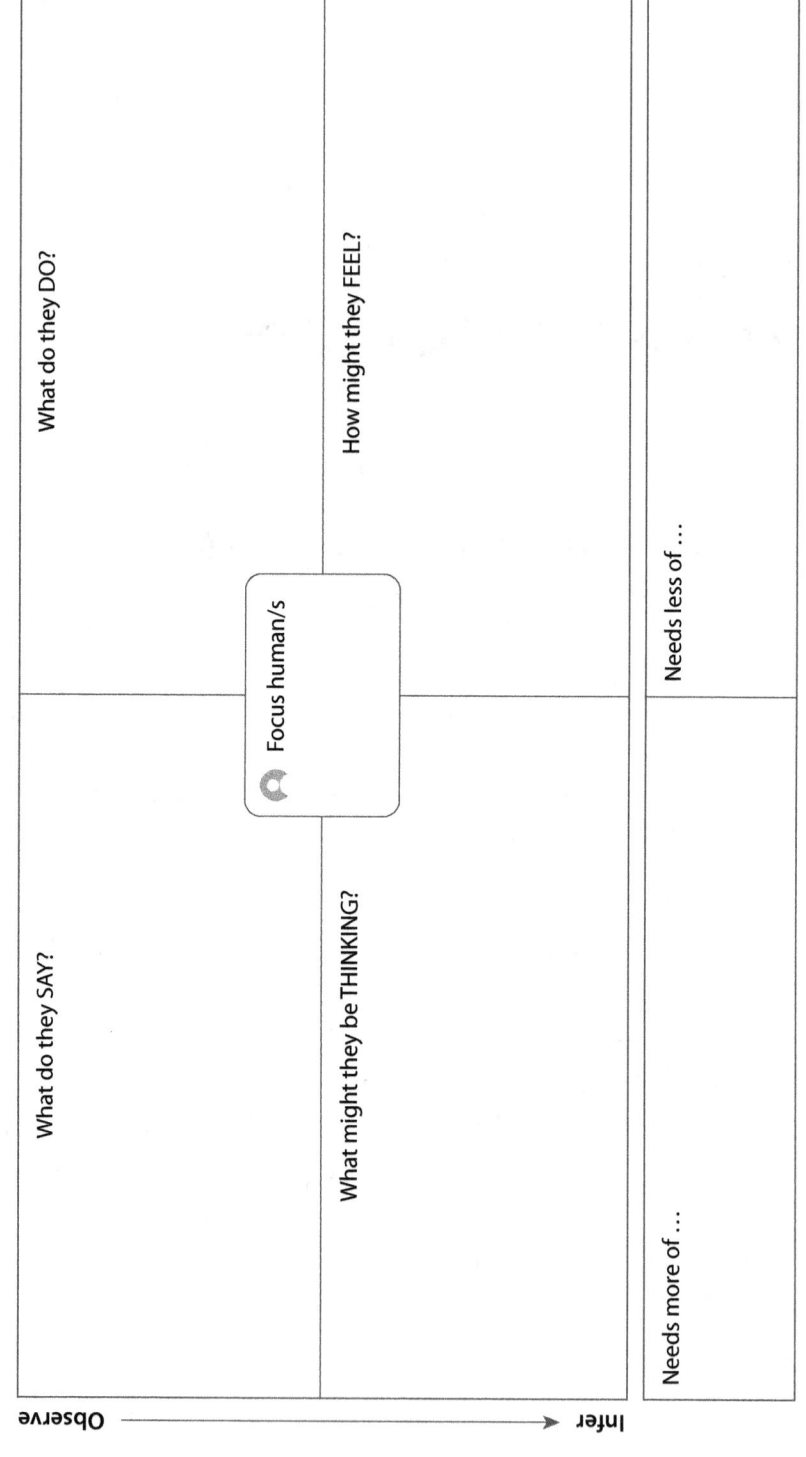

The connection conversation tool

As human beings, we are profound animals with the capacity to climb into each other's mental and emotional states. It's a powerful ability at our disposal, yet many of us underestimate it. Enter the Empathy Square tool. I remember running a session at a school once, and there was a teacher in his mid-fifties who was giving off some obvious signals that he didn't think he'd get anything out of this session. While the rest of the group was getting into the task, I went over and began a discussion with him about what was happening in his classes. He was having an issue with some Year 10 kids who were disengaged, disruptive and not putting in the effort. He shared that he dreaded the periods in the week when he was scheduled to teach that class and was frustrated with the students. We started working with the Empathy Square tool, describing what some of his Year 10 kids do and say, and inferring what they think and feel.

As this teacher transitioned into the 'think and feel' section, he experienced an incredible moment of insight about what was really going on, which paused his regular rhythm of frustration and allowed him to have a profound sense of the other's experience. At the end of the tool, he shared with me: 'The kids need me to engage relationally, reconnect and give them a fresh start. They just need some small wins, so they know they can actually make progress in this subject.' The reality is that if you can trigger in your own mind the emotional state of the person you're seeking to help, your brain is going to be much more likely to generate strategies and approaches that work for that person. Activating empathy doesn't necessarily mean you have a natural personal connection with someone; it means you care enough about the outcome to put in the emotional effort.

The Empathy Square supports teams in building a shared understanding and deepening their empathy by enabling them to see things from another person's perspective, especially students. It helps us slow down, step into someone else's shoes, and make more informed, human-centred decisions about what needs to change.

This tool is inspired by the Empathy Map concept originally developed by Dave Gray, the founder of XPLAN, and featured in his co-authored book *Gamestorming: A Playbook for Innovators, Rulebreakers, and Changemakers* (Gray et al., 2010). Similar empathy-based tools have also been advocated and popularised by the Stanford d.school, particularly through their human-centred design toolkits.

Empathy Square facilitator guidance

Preparation

Each member of the group can work on their own copy of the Empathy Square template. Alternatively, a shared large copy or wall poster version can be used. If using this format, group members can capture their individual thinking on sticky notes before adding them to the shared template.

Step 1: Orient the team

When focusing on an aspect of our teaching that isn't having the desired impact for students, it is often useful to surface human insights through empathising with the experiences of the students themselves.

The Empathy Square tool is all about seeing teaching through the eyes of the learner – using this tool, we contemplate how our teaching might be experienced by students, and we can then consider how to make changes to our practice. Let empathy drive you as you complete this activity, and keep it real. Empathy is about putting yourself in somebody else's shoes – in this case, your students' shoes.

Step 2: Identify which student/s you will focus on

Define a specific learning challenge area or context that you are going to focus the activity on (for example, students who aren't making progress with writing, students who are behaving poorly when transitioning from break time back into class, students who have missed more than 20 per cent of school days, or students who require further extension in mathematics). Ask each group member to bring to mind one specific student with whom they interact and can focus on during the tool. They should write this student's first name or initials in the middle of the Empathy Square.

Step 3: Complete the four questions

Each member of the group now completes the four key questions that are captured on the Empathy Square (Say, Do, Think, Feel). Each member can fill out their own template sheet or capture their responses on sticky notes.

Fill in the template through the following steps:

- Reflect and write what they 'Say' and 'Do' as learners when engaging in this learning area/process. These should be things you can see or hear (observable actions) – for example, they might say 'This is dumb' or 'I can't do this', or they might stay silent. They might begin the task and then stop within the first two minutes. Or they might automatically begin speaking with a class member to clarify what they are meant to be doing.

- Now infer what they might 'Think' and 'Feel' when being taught in this learning area. Attuning with empathy is crucial during this step, as we are trying to ascertain what these learners are 'most likely' thinking and feeling. For example, they might be thinking 'I'm not sure where to begin' or 'I really hope she doesn't call on me'. They might be feeling 'anxious' or 'frustrated'. During this step, you are trying to carefully consider what might be happening inside this student's head and heart and to connect with the student's feelings, frustrations and worries. If you don't feel like you can accurately infer at this stage, then feel free to put a '?' in the box to denote that you aren't sure yet. You might find the table of emotions below a helpful way of activating a broader set of terms to describe potential emotional states.

Emotions that might serve as helpful prompts for empathic reflection

They might feel...

- Joyful
- Happy
- Satisfied
- Hopeful
- Energised

- Interested
- Curious
- Excited
- Surprised
- Calm

- Relaxed
- Proud
- Pleased
- Delighted
- Triumphant

- Respected
- Valued
- Bored
- Confused
- Disillusioned
- Dismayed
- Anxious
- Worried
- Panicked
- Stressed
- Nervous
- Apprehensive
- Fearful
- Disappointed
- Sad
- Overwhelmed
- Pressured
- Lonely
- Isolated
- Unhappy
- Miserable
- Hopeless
- Ashamed
- Awkward
- Inferior
- Frustrated
- Annoyed
- Angry
- Infuriated
- Insulted

Step 4: Share insights

As a group, take time to each share your specific student responses while holding up your individual template, or by adding your sticky notes to the group template. You can use the following structure:

The student I have focused on is… (you may also choose to keep this anonymous).

- **Say** – I hear this student say things like…
- **Do** – I have observed that this student often…
- **Think** – I have inferred that the student might be thinking…
- **Feel** – I have inferred that the student might be feeling…

Discuss as a group what you've learned from the Empathy Square and where there were obvious similarities and differences across the specific learners discussed.

Seek to gain new insights into why these students are not yet making the desired progress in this outcome area. Place particular focus on the Feel box. Remember, emotions are the gateway to learning. Suppose students are not in the optimal emotional state: in that case, it is unlikely that they will be able to learn effectively. For example, it is almost impossible to engage in effective learning behaviours if you are feeling angry, anxious or afraid.

Top tip!

Wherever possible, inferences about what students might be thinking and feeling should be based on multiple observations, and you should be able to answer the question 'So what did you observe that makes you say that?' when you have made an inference. A word of caution: be careful not to treat inferences as facts.

Step 5: Explore adjustments

Now that you've surfaced a range of insights, discuss the adjustments you could make for particular students to improve their outcomes. Synthesise your thinking through the following questions and record your answers as a group:

- What have we learned about why these students are likely not making the desired progress?
- What specific learning needs have we uncovered?
- How might these human insights inform our next steps in working with these students?
    - What might these students need more of?
    - What might these students need less of?
    - What will we commit to trialling?

Assign action steps, responsibilities and a timeline as necessary.

Useful resource – the feelings wheel

In order to broaden the range of emotional vocabulary used, some team leaders find it useful to print off a few copies of the open-source feelings wheel. You can access this at https://feelingswheel.com/

Empathy Square example 1 – Understanding chronic absenteeism

School type	Group	How many people	Length of meeting
Low secondary	Cross-functional team	8	30 mins

At a mid-sized secondary school, a cross-disciplinary team had become increasingly concerned about a group of students in Years 8 and 9 with persistently low attendance. In each grade, over ten students had missed more than 30 per cent of school days in the first half of the year. Many had inconsistent patterns across different subjects, but some were disengaging more broadly. The school leadership team knew that unless they addressed the trend now, these students would struggle to stay on and succeed toward high school graduation.

Grace, the head teacher (wellbeing), pulled together a team that included year advisers, the deputy principal, a representative from the learning and support team, and three classroom teachers who taught these students across different subjects. She wanted to use the Empathy Square tool to help the group move beyond frustration and speculation, and instead step into a more thoughtful analysis of what might be going on beneath the surface.

Before they began, Grace framed up the discussion: 'This is about slowing down and really trying to see school through the eyes of our most disengaged students,' she said. 'Let's challenge our assumptions and look at the human experience behind the pattern of the data we can see.'

Each team member was given a printed Empathy Square template and a copy of the attendance snapshot showing absence rates for the ten focus students. Grace asked each person to pick one student they taught, or interacted with regularly, who was showing high non-attendance, and write their initials in the centre. 'Let's spend the first four minutes completing what we know they say and do when they are here. Then we'll try to infer what they might think and feel when they are at school or thinking about coming to school.'

To deepen the emotional and cognitive reflection, Grace displayed a prompt list of emotions, encouraging the team to use specific language to name the inferred internal states of the students.

One teacher wrote:

- **Say:** 'What's the point?' 'I'll probably get in trouble anyway.'
- **Do:** Arrives late, sits at the back, avoids eye contact, does not bring equipment.
- **Think:** 'I can't catch up now.' 'No one really notices if I'm here or not.'
- **Feel:** Overwhelmed, invisible, anxious, out of place.

Another noted:

- **Say:** 'This is boring.' 'Why are we even doing this?'
- **Do:** Skips the last period, never hands in homework, distracted on phone.
- **Think:** 'This isn't for me.' 'I'm not smart enough.' 'They expect me to fail.'
- **Feel:** Frustrated, ashamed, inferior, misunderstood.

After a few minutes of silent work, Grace invited a few people to share, gently asking, 'What do you think this student might be trying to tell us through their behaviour?' She also prompted, 'Where might we be unintentionally reinforcing the idea that school is a place they don't belong?'

The conversation brought out recurring patterns, including:

- A disconnect between students' cultural identity and the school environment
- Low self-concept about learning and academic ability
- Negative past experiences with teachers
- Overwhelm at returning after long absences without support to catch up
- Family responsibilities or instability interfering with routines.

To close, the group used the final reflection questions to consider how they might shift their approach:

- What might these students need more of?
    - Proactive connection and check-ins from key staff
    - Individual re-entry plans after absences
    - Smaller wins and achievable tasks to rebuild confidence
    - Stronger messages of high expectations and belief in success
    - Opportunities for cultural identity and voice to be valued.
- What might they need less of?
    - Impersonal roll-marking or punitive late processes
    - Overloaded catch-up work sent without explanation
    - Reprimands that assume laziness or disinterest
    - Low expectations masked as 'kindness' or avoidance
    - Exclusion from key activities or leadership roles.

The discussion helped the group shift from blame to curiosity. Grace thanked them for their depth of insight and encouraged each person to follow up with one small action for the student they focused on. She took photos of the completed empathy maps and summarised themes in a follow-up email. The team agreed to meet again in two weeks to build these insights into their attendance policies and practices. Later they ran a similar activity with the full staff before building a shared understanding of the practices to be used when supporting students with chronic absenteeism.

Empathy Square example 2 – Instruction coaching on classroom routines

School type	Group	How many people	Length of meeting
All school types	1:1 instructional coaching	2	45 mins

Layla, a first-year teacher, had been struggling with low-level disruption and disengagement, especially during transitions between classroom activities. She had recently spoken to the principal about how unsettled she felt in the role and how she dreaded the parts of the day when she had to regain control after movement or change. The leadership team acknowledged that stronger induction systems were needed and arranged for Judy, the school's instructional coach, to support Layla with practical strategies.

To begin their first session together, Judy chose to use the Empathy Square tool. Rather than jumping into solution mode, she wanted Layla to build insight into her students' internal states and the possible causes of their behaviours. 'Let's step into their shoes for a moment,' she said. 'The goal here is to see the classroom through their eyes so that we can choose strategies that actually work for them.'

They sat side by side at a shared table using a printed template. Judy used the three-point communication stance, keeping the focus on the student, not the teacher. To ease Layla into the session, Judy shared a personal story about how she used to fear one of her classes during the period on Thursdays, and how she once mistook student confusion for defiance and inadvertently escalated an interaction. Layla and Judy both laughed, and Layla's shoulders relaxed. There was a state of psychological safety and a shared task of improvement rather than judgment ahead.

Together, they identified a group of students who were consistently unsettled during transitions, whether that was entering the classroom, moving between group and independent tasks, or shifting into a different subject. Layla said, 'It's like they fall apart the second I ask them to move.'

Judy asked her to choose one specific student as a focal point. They then filled out the Empathy Square together, starting with observable behaviour.

- **Say:** 'Do we have to do this?' 'This is dumb.'
- **Do:** Talks to peers during instructions, fiddles with materials, takes several minutes to get started.
- **Think:** 'This is when no one's watching, so I can chill.' 'I don't want to get this wrong in front of everyone.'
- **Feel:** Energised, unsure, distractible.

Judy asked, 'If you were that student at that moment, what might you need more of?' Layla paused, then said, 'Clearer expectations. A moment to focus. Maybe even a job to do straight away.'

They completed a few more Empathy Squares for other students, each time pausing to move from what they could see and hear to what they might infer. One student was described as 'quiet but slow to start', and when Layla reflected, she noted that he might be nervous, unsure how to begin, and afraid of doing the wrong thing.

Across the squares, common themes emerged. Many students seemed energised and social during transitions, but also uncertain, awkward or unmotivated. Layla realised that her own instructions were often vague ('Get ready for the next activity') and that she wasn't following up with enough precision or praise for positive transitions.

Judy introduced the concept of learning routines and reminded Layla that transitions are teachable moments. 'You're not just moving between tasks. You're teaching focus, listening and readiness to learn. And that takes structure.'

They co-designed a new transition routine using Judy's routine-building sequence:

1. Explain the purpose: 'This helps us switch gears quickly and calmly.'
2. Describe what success looks and doesn't look like.
3. Model the routine and rehearse it with students.
4. Narrate success and correct students calmly but clearly.

They wrote a simple script together: 'When I say "reset", you close your book, take a breath, face the front and wait silently. If you're ready early, show me with your hands folded or a thumbs up.'

Judy also recommended using pre-correction, short cues like 'Get ready for reset', and specific praise to reinforce success: 'Thanks, Alex, that was a calm and fast reset.'

To close the session, they returned to the Empathy Squares and asked:

- 'What do these students need more of?'
    - Specific routines
    - Clarity
    - Positive recognition
    - Safe ways to participate.
- 'What do these students need less of?'
    - Vague expectations
    - Negative public correction
    - Assumed compliance without modelling.

Layla looked down at the page and said quietly, 'This feels doable now. I've been correcting too late instead of teaching what I want to see. This gives me something to build on.' They agreed to a plan: Judy would model the routine in Layla's class the next day during a co-teaching session. The next week, after Layla had had some time to practise in the class, Judy would observe Layla and provide some feedback. They would debrief and work out what to work on next.

Empathy Square example 3 – Building insight about students with additional learning needs

School type	Group	How many people	Length of meeting
Lower secondary	Teacher team	6	30 mins

Fatima, a team leader, had noticed a concerning pattern in the behavioural data across her stage team. One student in particular had accumulated a high number of negative behaviour incidents across multiple classes. Ravi, a newer teacher in the team, was responsible for a significant portion of the referrals and was becoming increasingly frustrated with the student's disruptions and lack of engagement.

Fatima had taught the same student the previous year. She knew he had ADHD and a trauma history, but also knew he could thrive under the right conditions. Ravi, on the other hand, tended to approach classroom behaviour with a strong emphasis on compliance and control. Fatima recognised that a one-on-one conversation might feel too pointed or uncomfortable, so she decided to use the Empathy Square in a group setting, allowing for shared reflection and modelling.

She opened the session by framing the purpose. 'We want to explore some of the patterns of behaviour that we are experiencing across our classes. This isn't about blame,' she said. 'It's about slowing down and really considering how some of our most complex students might be experiencing our classroom environments. We're here to make room for new thinking and hopefully gain some fresh insights.'

Each teacher received printed behavioural data and a blank Empathy Square template. Fatima asked them to choose one student they had recorded multiple negative incidents for, and write the student's initials in the centre of the page. 'We'll take four minutes to work individually,' she said. 'Focus first on what the student says and does – what you've actually seen or heard. Then shift into the harder part – what they might be thinking or feeling.'

To support depth, Fatima displayed a range of emotion vocabulary on the screen, including both surface and complex states like anxious, ashamed, energised and overwhelmed.

After the silent thinking time, Fatima invited a few volunteers to share their squares. This modelling helped set a reflective tone. Then it was Ravi's turn. His square read:

- **Say:** 'This is dumb.' 'You can't make me.'
- **Do:** Wanders the room, taps others on the shoulder, refuses to begin tasks.
- **Think:** 'I don't get this.' 'If I try, I'll probably get it wrong.' 'Everyone thinks I'm a problem.'
- **Feel:** Embarrassed, frustrated, hopeless, threatened.

Fatima gently prompted: 'If this is what he's thinking and feeling, what might that tell us about the behaviours you're seeing?' Ravi paused. 'He probably feels like he's already failed before he starts. So pushing back is easier than trying and struggling in front of everyone.'

Another teacher noted that the student is often energised and loud when the task first begins, then shifts into avoidance once work time starts. 'That energy might look disruptive,' she said, 'but maybe it's masking worry or overwhelm.'

Fatima helped the group reflect more deeply. 'We know ADHD affects executive functioning – things like focus, initiation and task-switching. But trauma also shapes how safe a student feels in a room. That combo is huge. So the question is: What does this student actually need from us?'

They turned to the closing reflection questions:

- What does this student need more of?
    - Predictable routines and visual cues
    - Warm, relational connection and positive feedback
    - Scaffolded instructions, broken into smaller steps
    - Non-verbal check-ins and private redirections
    - Opportunities for success early in the lesson.

- What does this student need less of?
  - Public corrections or repeated reprimands
  - Unstructured or overly long independent work time
  - Ambiguous instructions or last-minute changes
  - High cognitive overload through multi-step tasks without scaffolding
  - Assumptions that behaviour equals defiance.

Ravi reflected quietly, then spoke. 'I think I've been expecting him to just fall in line without doing the work to get him there.'

Following the session, Ravi initiated a meeting with the learning and support team. Together, they co-developed a set of classroom strategies tailored to the student's needs, including the use of visual routines, a quiet break card, and task scaffolds with progress prompts. They also agreed to explore Tier 3 intervention supports to address the student's missed foundational learning.

Fatima followed up with an email thanking the team for the depth of reflection. 'When we look through a student's eyes,' she wrote, 'we remember that behaviour is often communication. Today we got clearer on what this student might be trying to say, and what we can do next.'

TOOL 2
DEEPER REASONS

Explore why students might be struggling to make progress

The Deeper Reasons tool enables a structured conversation that helps your team pause and explore the underlying reasons why a student is experiencing a particular challenge. It stops everyone from jumping to quick fixes, so you can work on the real underlying problem/s.

Use this tool to:
- slow down the analysis of the 'problem that needs to be solved' to support student progress, in order to think more critically
- identify the underlying reasons that might be holding back student learning
- help you and your team think more deeply about the reasons why students are not yet being successful in the target outcome area or with the specific strategies currently being used
- go beyond surface-level descriptions and get to the heart of the issue.

Deeper Reasons

Surface-level challenge statement: The challenge we are facing is …

Reason 1	Reason 2	Reason 3

Why do we think this is happening?

Understand and reflect:
What do we now understand to be the most important underlying cause of this challenge?
Which of these underlying causes are within our influence?
What questions remain unanswered – and how might we explore them?

The problem-framing conversation tool

We all know the feeling: there's a student learning issue or a frustrating pattern in our school data, and our instinct is to jump straight into action mode. But sometimes our 'solutions' don't work – not because we didn't try hard enough, but because we were solving the wrong problem. The Deeper Reasons tool is designed to slow us down and help us think more clearly before we leap.

I remember a session where a team was frustrated that writing results weren't improving despite substantial teacher effort. As we worked through the Deeper Reasons tool, it emerged that the issue wasn't student growth mindset and motivation in writing, as was originally assumed when formulating their initial response – it was that students lacked clarity on success criteria and had no models to learn from. You could feel the energy shift as the group realised they'd been trying to 'motivate' students who simply didn't know what good writing looked like. That insight changed everything.

I've seen other teams who completely agreed that there was a problem, such as lagging maths results, come to realise, through this tool, that among themselves they had totally different beliefs about the cause. Some pointed to maths anxiety, others to fluency gaps, and others to unclear curriculum sequencing. It's in these moments, when new perspectives emerge and assumptions are tested, that powerful insights are revealed.

Most of our days are filled with swift decisions made while running at a rapid pace. However, when we're dealing with complex challenges or persistent problems, we need something different: a moment to pause and truly reflect. The Deeper Reasons tool helps us do just that. It stops us from jumping into surface-level fixes and instead creates a space for teams to co-develop a working theory of what's really going on. As Viviane Robinson reminds us in her work, it is crucial that we deeply understand the current context before initiating a change (Robinson, 2017). Just as great doctors begin with a thorough history before making a diagnosis, great educators need to pause and understand the deeper causes before rushing to solutions.

This tool isn't about action planning. It's about surfacing unspoken assumptions and understanding the real drivers of the patterns you're seeing. As Mark Twain supposedly said, 'It ain't what you don't know that gets you into trouble. It's what you know for sure that just ain't so'. You'll be surprised what emerges when you give your team the chance to slow down and go deeper.

This tool is informed by root cause analysis practices such as the '5 Whys' technique, and aligns with the emphasis on problem definition and causal thinking found in improvement science.

Deeper Reasons facilitator guidance

Preparation

If possible, it is useful to define a specific challenge ahead of the session. The facilitator could also gather any relevant information or data about the challenge so that it is available to refer to during the session if needed.

Each member of the group can work on their own copy of the Deeper Reasons template. Alternatively, a shared large copy or wall poster version can be used. If using this larger format, group members can capture their individual thinking on sticky notes before adding them to the shared template.

> **Framing the work together**
>
> Together, we'll be digging deep to try to get to the bottom of a problem that we are facing. We are here to explore and investigate, not blame, judge or jump to a solution. During this session, we are going to more deeply understand why this group of students is not yet making the desired progress in this learning outcome area. The goal is not to come up with new solutions, but rather to more deeply understand the situation that might be leading to the current pattern of student engagement and outcomes.

Step 1: State the challenge

To begin, one person should provide a basic, surface-level description of the challenge you're exploring. Together, you can then spend some time answering any clarifying questions about the nature of the problem.

- The challenge we're facing is ...
- The problem we are trying to understand is ...
- An issue that keeps coming up is ...
- Who is experiencing this problem?
- What signs point to there being a problem?
- Why do we think this problem is worth deeper analysis?
- In what circumstances is this problem occurring? In what circumstances does it not occur?

Write a simple surface-level challenge statement at the top of the Deeper Reasons template. The group needs to keep the discussion focused on understanding the deeper reasons contributing to or causing this challenge for the rest of the session.

Step 2: Generate a list of reasons

Each group member generates two or three key potential reasons that could be contributing to the identified challenge. Think about:

- Potential reasons that stem from student actions, decisions, relationships or past learning experiences
- Potential reasons that are connected to teacher practice, beliefs or resources. To put it another way, 'How might we as teachers be contributing to the current pattern of student behaviour, engagement and outcomes?'

Each reason should be written on a separate sticky note. For example:

- Students don't understand basic sentence structure.
- Teachers struggle with motivating students in this target outcome area.
- We are not confident with the materials.

- We are unsure about the best teaching strategy.
- We are not feeling inspired or motivated to teach this weak and disjointed unit of work.

Step 3: Cluster the reasons

The goal of this step is to cluster some of the potential key reasons developed by individual team members into groups.

1. The first team member shares their first sticky note.
2. The second team member then takes their first sticky note and determines if the reason on the sticky note is similar or different.
3. If the reason is similar, they place it beside the one that is already up. If the reason is different, they create a new cluster.
4. This is repeated until all of the sticky notes from all of the team members are up on the wall. (Keep things moving quickly at this stage and avoid getting bogged down.)
5. The team members look at the clusters that they have created on the wall and select what they agree to be the three most important potential reason clusters.
6. If they can't come to a simple agreement, they vote on the reasons to move forward.

Step 4: Find the deeper reason/s

The team now writes each of the three key potential reasons in the top boxes on the template (Reason 1, Reason 2, Reason 3) or on chart paper if space allows, starting with the first reason, then working through the other boxes of the template.

1. The facilitator asks, 'Why do we think this is happening?' and when the team comes up with a possible deeper reason, this is written down in the next box below.
2. The facilitator then says, 'Let's go deeper – why do we think [last answer] is happening?' The team comes up with a deeper reason, which is written underneath.

3. The facilitator then says, 'Let's get to the root of the issue – why do we think [last answer] is happening?' The team comes up with an even deeper reason, which is written underneath.

Repeat this process for each of the three top reasons that you originally generated as a team. At times you might find these alternative question frames helpful:

1. What caused this... ?
2. What led to... ?
3. What are the conditions under which... occurred?
4. What contributed to this... ?

Variation

If working with a larger group, you can break into sub-teams to do this step. After completing the template, come back to see what 'deeper reasons' each sub-team has ended up with.

Note: For some of the reasons generated, you will not find it possible or useful to go down to three deeper levels. Just work through as many as you can. At other times, you may find you need to keep asking 'why' beyond the first three levels.

Step 5: Understand and reflect

Consider each of the 'deepest reasons' you have generated. Discuss the synthesis and reflection questions at the bottom of the template as a group:

- What do we now understand to be the most important underlying causes of this challenge?
- Which of these underlying causes are within our influence?
- What questions remain unanswered – and how might we explore them?

Further questions to go deeper:

- What can we learn from this?

- What do we believe are the one or two deeper reasons that are *most* likely to be leading to the pattern of student engagement, behaviour and learning that we are seeing?
- How might we need to reframe how we have been talking about this challenge/problem?
- Which 'deeper reasons' can we impact through the design of our teaching and direct relationships with students?
- Which deeper reasons might we be able to influence through other strategies, routines and processes?

Assign action steps, responsibilities and a timeline as necessary.

Prompts to discover potential underlying reasons

Student	- Regularity of student attendance
	- Student cognitive engagement and focus
	- Student prior learning/knowledge
	- Student vocabulary
	- Student literacy/numeracy levels
	- Student perception of student–teacher relationships
	- Student metacognition and learning strategies
	- Peer effects in the learning environment
	- Student efficacy beliefs
	- Levels of student effort and deliberate practice
	- Student wellbeing
	- Levels of belonging and connection
	- Student sleep quality
	- Student food intake
	- Student frequency of physical movement
Teacher	- Teacher level of knowledge of and confidence in content/curriculum/ syllabus
	- Teacher energy and passion when teaching in this area
	- Classroom management practices and routines

| Teacher (cont.) | - Extent to which a positive climate for learning has been developed
- Quality of teacher–student relationships
- Quality of programming and lesson planning
- Number of hours allocated and intensity of focus
- Lesson clarity, learning intentions and success criteria
- Quality and relevance of summative assessment tasks
- Level of expectations for all students to achieve at a high level
- Use of evidence to assess students' prior knowledge
- Consistency of evidence-informed teaching strategies
- Use of assessment to track student progress
- Use of feedback to help students know their next steps in learning |
|---|---|
| Other factors | **Leadership:**
- Insufficient clarity about expectations
- Lack of relational trust
- Lack of direct support
- Insufficient follow-up and accountability of staff about core expectations
- Low levels of trust

School processes:
- Insufficient professional learning opportunities
- No regularly tracking of data
- Lack of resourcing
- Lack of school-wide policies and approaches

Family:
- Parental/caregiver expectations for attendance and achievement
- Parental/caregiver support with learning and homework
- Provision of enriching activities
- Active modelling of reading in the home |

Deeper Reasons example 1 – Exploring Year 5 reading decline

School type	Group	How many people	Length of meeting
Primary	Whole staff	22	60 mins

Following the national assessment results, Susan, the principal, identified a recurring trend: while Year 3 reading scores consistently exceeded the state average, Year 5 results showed a relative decline. This was evident both in terms of overall expected growth and in comparison to schools with similar Year 3 profiles. The dip was not limited to a single cohort. It was a persistent pattern that required collective analysis and action.

While Susan had a few hypotheses, she knew it would be more effective for the staff to reason through the problem together. If the staff could collectively explore the evidence and arrive at their own conclusions, any change would be more sustainable. She introduced the Deeper Reasons tool to help the team move beyond surface-level explanations and into the heart of the challenge.

She opened the session with a clear statement of purpose: 'We're seeing strong Year 3 reading outcomes followed by a notable drop by Year 5. This is not just in absolute terms, but also in how we compare against schools similar to ours. Today's question is: What might be contributing to this pattern, and what sits beneath it?'

To frame the work, she reminded staff of two of their shared collaboration norms: 'Make room for new thinking' and 'Invite healthy challenge'. 'This session is not about judging or evaluating. It's not just about reaching a consensus or making excuses. The goal is deeper thinking about what is happening for our students, so that we can understand the real problems we will need to solve together.'

She placed teachers into mixed-grade trio groups to broaden the perspective and support deeper discussion. Each trio received a large copy of the Deeper Reasons template and a printout showing the reading data trends for Years 3 and 5.

Before beginning the group work, Susan invited participants to take five minutes of individual silent reflection to generate their ideas about what might be the key reasons driving this trend. She asked teachers to jot down two or three sticky notes, drawing on their recent professional learning on effective reading instruction.

Each trio then began working through their template. Teachers took turns sharing one sticky note at a time and discussed whether it aligned with others or introduced a new line of thinking. Once clusters of the core reasons were established, the trios were guided to select three key reasons and used the template to unpack them vertically:

- 'Why might this be happening?'
- 'What is sitting underneath that?'
- 'What else is contributing?'

In one group, a reasoning ladder unfolded like this:

- Surface-level reason: Year 5 students struggle with deeper comprehension tasks.
- Why? Teachers are not explicitly teaching strategies like predicting, summarising and visualising.
- Why? Staff confidence is higher in phonics and early decoding than in comprehension instruction.
- Why? Professional learning has focused on K–2 foundations, with limited follow-up in the middle years.

After 25 minutes, Susan brought the groups back together and invited each trio to post their completed templates on the wall. The front wall of the room became a gallery of deeper thinking. Teachers rotated and read one another's reasoning chains, noting similarities, tensions and new ideas.

Susan then led a whole-group reflection using synthesis prompts:

- 'What patterns are we seeing again and again?'
- 'What deeper reasons are standing out across the room?'

The discussion surfaced a number of themes:

- A significant drop in reading volume and motivation after Year 3, especially a decline in independent reading of chapter books with complex syntax and abstract ideas
- Lack of explicit instruction in comprehension strategies such as inferencing, summarising and making predictions
- Gaps in staff confidence and shared pedagogy for teaching comprehension and vocabulary beyond decoding
- A lack of embedded formative assessment tools for tracking progress in comprehension, despite strong assessment practices for decoding and fluency in the earlier grades of primary.

Susan closed the session with a focused reflection:

- 'Which of these deeper reasons are within our control?'
- 'Where might we focus first to create a different trajectory for our students?'

Susan photographed each group's reasoning map, posted a summary to the team portal, and shared some ideas for selected readings for follow-up, including *The Reading Mind* by Daniel Willingham (2017) and *Improving Literacy in Key Stage 2: Guidance Report* from the Education Endowment Foundation (2018).

When she asked teachers for some feedback, they described the session as non-judgmental and refreshing, with one staff member noting, 'I finally feel like we're naming the real work we need to focus on.'

Deeper Reasons example 2 – Understanding declining participation in PE and sport

School type	Group	How many people	Length of meeting
Secondary	Physical education department	8	40 mins

The PE team had become increasingly concerned about low student participation across the school's sports and physical education programs. Attendance at weekly sports afternoons and whole-school carnival days was dropping, and even during regular PE lessons, many students were disengaged or arriving unprepared. Teachers reported a growing pattern of students opting out, either through passive resistance or by failing to bring their gear. The team wanted to halt this slide before it became normalised. They believed that helping students to re-engage with physical activity was essential, not only for their health and wellbeing but also for developing confidence, motivation and positive peer relationships.

Paul, the head of department, introduced the Deeper Reasons tool to guide a shared exploration. 'This is about more than skipping sport or forgetting a uniform,' he said. 'We need to look more closely at the culture we are building around PE, and what is making it harder for students to opt in.'

He began by reminding the team of their shared norms: Stick to what matters, make room for new thinking and invite healthy challenge. 'Let's be honest about what we are seeing and what we might be contributing to. This is a space for open thinking, not blame.'

Each teacher received three sticky notes and five minutes of silent thinking time. Paul gave a clear prompt: 'Think about the students who are regularly disengaged or absent. What do you believe are the key reasons they are opting out?'

Once the notes were written, the team took turns sharing their ideas, grouping similar reasons and discussing differences. After reviewing the clusters, they agreed on three key patterns to explore more deeply:

1. Students don't feel good enough to participate.
2. Students are not interested or motivated.
3. There is a lack of consistency in how participation is expected and followed up.

Paul guided the team through deeper questioning and captured the responses at each level of the tool. The completed tool captured the following deeper reasons and insights:

Reason 1: Students don't feel good enough to participate	Reason 2: Why might students be disengaged or uninterested?	Reason 3: Why might there be inconsistent expectations?
Many struggle to experience success or recognition in PE.	Some students do not see the relevance of PE to their lives.	Staff vary in how they follow up on non-participation, with few consequences.
Activities often favour already-confident or athletic students.	The program offers limited variety and choice. It is the same set of sports.	Parents and students are not sure that it matters whether they participate or not.
Teachers are not regularly breaking down and developing the specific sub-skills required to be successful in specific sports.	Students feel that sport is only for the competitive or highly able. They would prefer to opt out.	There is a lack of clear communication from the school, and insufficient follow-up with students and parents for non-participation.

Paul paused the discussion and asked, 'Which of these deeper issues are within our influence, and where might we focus first?'

The team agreed on three practical next steps:

1. Run a short anonymous student survey to better understand how students perceive sport and PE
2. Begin a round of peer lesson observations, focusing on inclusion through explicit instruction, teacher praise and encouragement, and helping students experience success
3. Provide consistent follow-up and a clear message to parents about expectations around engagement in sport with the key dates for the term ahead.

As the session closed, Paul thanked the team for their honesty and focus. One teacher summed it up well: 'That was a really helpful chat. We're not just blaming the kids for being lazy. We're talking about how to rebuild value and belonging in PE. That's exactly why I got into PE teaching in the first place.'

TOOL 3
OUTCOME HEAT MAP

Visualise the most important and hard-to-teach learning outcomes to focus on

The Outcome Heat Map is a prioritisation tool that brings clarity when everything feels important. It helps your team map out what's most essential for students to learn and what's hardest for them to grasp, so you can focus your teaching improvement efforts where it matters most.

Use this tool to:

- determine the essential learning outcomes in a particular subject, topic or curriculum area
- identify outcomes that are hard to teach but important for students to learn
- prioritise focus outcomes for intentional preparation and professional development.

Outcome Heat Map

What specific subject, domain, learning area or unit are we focusing on?

	Harder to teach	
Essential to learn		
Important to learn		
	Easier to teach	

The learning prioritisation conversation tool

When everything feels important, it's hard to know where to focus. I've worked with so many teams who hit that wall – overloaded programs, jam-packed unit plans, and lessons full of good intentions but unclear priorities. The Outcome Heat Map is the go-to tool for moments like these. It brings clarity by helping us ask two deceptively simple questions: 'What's essential for students to learn?' and 'What's hardest for us to teach?'

This tool is especially powerful at the start of a year, term or unit. It shifts us from trying to cover everything to focusing our planning and practice on what matters most. It's not about cutting corners – it's about sharpening focus and bringing collective energy to the teaching moments that really count for students' long-term developmental pathways.

The 'Harder to teach' category is where the real gold is. It reveals where we might be working hard, but students still aren't getting it. I remember a conversation with a passionate primary teacher using this tool to reflect on writing. He'd placed 'teaching sentence types' in the 'Easier to teach' box. I asked why. He said, 'Because I understand it, it's straightforward to me.' I followed up: 'What does your data say about how many of your students deeply understand it and apply it confidently?' He paused. 'Oh... a lot of them still have absolutely no idea.' That moment of reflection shifted everything. The issue wasn't *his* level of understanding – it was how difficult the concept was for students to grasp, despite his best efforts. That's what professional discussions about what is 'essential to learn and harder to teach' are all about: the things that we teach, but many students don't learn.

I've never run this tool with a teacher team without a rich conversation surfacing about specific content areas that just don't seem to stick. As a former secondary science teacher, I remember how often students could complete the steps in a structured lab experiment but still couldn't explain basic features of experimental design, like identifying independent and dependent variables. Experimental design is clearly essential to learn for foundational science understanding, and, for me at least, it was harder to teach.

The Outcome Heat Map tool invites openness and professional vulnerability. Teams regularly share frustrations and failures, but they also walk away with a clear focus on collective planning and creative problem-solving. Once you've identified what sits in the top-right quadrant – 'Essential to learn, Harder to teach' – you can dig into research, identify more effective strategies and collaborative design and test new lesson sequences together.

Outcome Heat Map facilitator guidance

Preparation

Provide an individual Outcome Heat Map template to each team member, or use a larger version or wall poster copy as a shared group template to capture thinking. This tool can also be drawn on a whiteboard or butcher's paper. Write the team's broad learning area along the top and then add labels to each box in the matrix ('Easier to teach', 'Harder to teach', 'Essential to learn', 'Important to learn').

The team leader may wish to have the curriculum, syllabus outlines, scope and sequence – or a specific learning continuum – available for the team to refer to.

Step 1: Identify a broad learning outcome area

To begin, state a broad learning outcome area that will be the focus for this analysis. This may be framed in terms of a broad skill or content area, a specific unit of work, or a period of time, such as over the next month or term – for example: 'Teaching essay writing', 'Developing phonics knowledge', 'Big ideas in numeracy development', 'Teaching the immune system'.

Note: If your group members do not have a shared teaching agenda, they can work through the shared steps together, but focus on their own individual content area.

Step 2: Break it down into discrete learning outcomes

The team works to develop a list of discrete learning outcomes that fit within the broader learning outcome area identified. Each specific outcome should be written on a separate sticky note.

Try to write each outcome as a specific thing you want students to know, understand and/or be able to do.

Step 3: Identify the outcomes that are 'Essential to learn'

The team then takes the sticky notes and places them on the matrix according to their relative level of importance for students to learn (from 'Important' to 'Essential') and level of difficulty to teach (from 'Easier' to 'Harder').

Start by sorting the discrete learning outcomes into the 'Important' and 'Essential' boxes within the matrix by using some of these prompts:

- Which ones do we think are the most important outcomes for students to grasp?
- What are the outcomes that are threshold concepts in the learning progression?
- Which outcomes, if they are not attained by students, will cause them substantial challenges later on in their learning?
- What are the outcomes here that often positively unlock accelerated progress in other areas?

Keep moving the notes until you've got an agreement about which box they belong in. It is natural to want to put all of the outcomes as 'Essential'. But try to be strict, and aim for the minimum number of outcomes in the 'Essential to learn' category.

Step 4: Sort out the outcomes that are 'Harder to teach'

From here, shift your attention to the 'Easier to teach' and 'Harder to teach' boxes, moving some of the sticky notes to the right, as appropriate. 'Harder to teach' refers to the success rate teachers have in being able to secure learning in this area. It does not necessarily refer to whether a teacher understands the learning concept or not, but is more about whether they can teach it to their students with a high degree of success. 'Harder to teach' areas are intrinsically more difficult for students to grasp and often require intentional instructional sequencing and multiple ways of explaining and modelling.

Consider these questions:

- Which important outcomes do we teach that many students do not actually learn?
- When marking assessments and reviewing student work, what challenges often emerge for students year after year?
- In which outcomes do we notice students often struggling to grasp the concept or take the next steps?
- For which outcomes do we feel we have an insufficient set of teaching strategies to support all students to make progress?

Healthy debate is encouraged here. Even if team members agree, the facilitator should encourage the team to justify their placement of outcomes on the matrix and discuss their 'relative' importance and difficulty. You should feel encouraged to share the evidence or experiences that led to your suggestions for what goes where on the template.

Step 5: Focus and plan next actions

The team should then focus on all of the sticky notes in the upper-right 'Essential to learn'/'Harder to teach' box and consider the next steps. Here are some guiding questions:

- Given our diverse classroom teaching experiences, to what extent do we agree on the outcomes in the top right box?
- What research-based ideas could inform a new approach to teaching this outcome?
- What actions should we take in our unit/lesson planning and resource development?
- How might we be able to lift our capacity through engaging in professional learning?

- What adjustments to our classroom teaching practice could we make that will differ from previous years? What different approaches do we think would be more effective?
- How can we better help students productively struggle and make progress through these outcomes?
- How could we use assessment to check student progress in these areas?
- How might we be able to move through a cycle of collaborative planning, teaching and observation to co-design a more successful approach?

Outcome Heat Map example 1 – Clarifying priorities for writing instruction

School type	Group	How many people	Length of meeting
Secondary	English teaching team	10	45 mins

Based on national assessment benchmarks and internal student work samples, the school's English department had identified writing as an area needing deeper focus. Despite well-structured units, student progress had not shifted in some critical areas. Tom, the new head of English, decided to use the Outcome Heat Map tool to help the team clarify where to direct their planning focus.

In preparation, Tom drew the Outcome Heat Map on a large whiteboard before the session. He labelled the vertical axis from bottom to top: 'Important to learn → Essential to learn', and the horizontal axis from left to right: 'Easier to teach → Harder to teach'.

He opened the session, helping the team to understand why they would be using the tool to explore writing outcomes: 'We've all been working hard to improve writing outcomes. Today, we're going to collectively consider which of the outcomes we're attempting to teach seem to be most difficult for our students to learn. This tool will help us focus our planning adjustments where they can make the biggest difference.'

Before starting, Tom reminded the group of one of their shared norms: 'Invite healthy challenge'. He added, 'We won't all see these writing outcomes the same way – and that's the point. Let's be open about what we find hard to teach, and try to provide real examples from what we're each experiencing in the classroom.'

Each teacher received sticky notes and was given two minutes of solo thinking time. 'List the specific knowledge or skills students need to be confident writers,' Tom said. 'Think about what you teach, and where students typically succeed or struggle.' Some of the outcomes generated were grouped into the following clusters:

- Sentence-level control
- Paragraph structure and cohesion

- Clarity of purpose and audience awareness
- Spelling fluency
- Grammar knowledge and application
- Academic vocabulary and precision
- Text structure and organisation
- Planning and outlining ideas before writing
- Revising for clarity, coherence and impact
- Use of language features for effect.

Next, the group moved into the first phase of sorting: How essential is each outcome? Tom guided the conversation using key prompts:

- 'Which outcomes are threshold concepts in writing?'
- 'Which ones, if missed, hold students back later on?'
- 'Which ones unlock progress in other aspects of writing?'

They then shifted focus to the horizontal axis, on how hard each outcome is to teach. Tom prompted:

- 'Which outcomes do we teach every year but students still struggle with?'
- 'Where do we lack clear strategies or shared models?'

Sticky notes began to move across the grid. Tom asked, 'Can someone capture those insights before we forget them?' A nominated scribe added notes directly to the whiteboard about some of the reasons given.

By the end of the sort, a few specific outcomes were clearly positioned in the top-right quadrant. Tom facilitated a focused reflection: 'Let's concentrate here for our next collaborative planning sessions. These are essential, and we don't yet have consistently strong approaches for teaching them.'

He asked the team:

- 'What adjustments to our teaching or modelling might make a difference?'
- 'Are there unit sequences we could redesign with these outcomes in mind?'

- 'What planning support or professional learning might help us shift this?'

At the end of the session, Tom photographed the completed map and shared it with the team, along with a short follow-up email outlining the focus areas and the following meeting dates. He also sent links to recent research by the Education Endowment Foundation (2019) on literacy and resources on the 'Writing Revolution' approach (Hochman & Wexler, 2017).

Outcome Heat Map example 2 – Focusing planning on hard-to-teach maths concepts

School type	Group	How many people	Length of meeting
Upper primary	Grades 5–6 teacher team	6	40 mins

Nerida, the Stage 3 assistant principal, wanted to deepen her team's focus on core mathematical understanding. She used the Outcome Heat Map to help the team clarify which concepts were most essential – and most difficult to teach well.

Before the session, Nerida drew the matrix on a large piece of butcher's paper. She labelled the vertical axis from bottom to top: 'Important to learn → Essential to learn', and the horizontal axis from left to right: 'Easier to teach → Harder to teach'. She also printed and cut out a list of key mathematical concepts drawn from their curriculum and recent assessments, including topics like place value, fractions, geometric reasoning, chance, spatial structure and multiplicative thinking.

She opened the session by naming the purpose. 'We're not here to cover every outcome,' she said. 'We're here to focus on the concepts that matter most, and that we know are hard to secure. This isn't just about content coverage, it's about where we focus our collaborative planning effort to make the most impact.'

To frame the conversation, she reminded the group of one of their shared collaboration norms: 'Stick to what matters.' She added, 'Let's resist the urge to map everything – our goal is clarity.'

Each teacher spent two minutes individually reviewing the list and categorising concepts into one of two categories: 'Important to learn' or 'Essential to learn'.

Nerida prompted:

- 'Which of these are threshold concepts, ideas that are crucial for later learning?'
- 'Which ones cause long-term issues if students don't grasp them?'

Once the team had shared and debated the placements, they began sorting the same outcomes along the 'Easier to teach → Harder to teach' axis. Discussion quickly centred on multiplication and division.

'We all teach this year after year,' one teacher said, 'but many students still don't really understand what division is, nor its relationship with writing fractions.' Another added that they struggled to model different strategies effectively: 'I don't feel confident with using arrays or area models.'

Nerida encouraged the team to unpack what made these concepts harder to teach:

- 'Is the difficulty about student misconceptions?'
- 'Is it about how we model or sequence the ideas?'
- 'Where does our current approach break down?'

Together, they discussed several core challenges:

- Students overgeneralise rules (for example, 'multiplication makes things bigger').
- Perhaps strategies have been taught procedurally, without underlying reasoning.
- There's limited use of representations such as arrays, bar models, or number lines in our units of work.

Nerida prompted a team member to act as scribe and capture the richness of the discussion and insights. By the end of the sort, multiplication and division sat clearly in the top-right quadrant: 'Essential to learn' and 'Harder to teach'.

To close the session, Nerida guided the team toward next steps:

- 'If this is where we focus, what planning changes are needed?'
- 'What further reading or professional learning might help?'

The team agreed to use their upcoming half-day curriculum planning session to:

- Co-design a series of lessons on multiplicative reasoning using arrays, number lines and bar models

- Build in diagnostic questions targeting common misconceptions
- Identify one task per week that would develop fluency.

As one teacher said as they closed out the session, 'This gave us a way to move from "we know this is a problem" to actually doing something practical about it'. Nerida shared the photographed map via their Microsoft Teams group and added a resource bundle, incorporating evidence-informed guidance (Evidence for Learning, 2020), which included examples of misconceptions, worked examples and suggested visuals to support conceptual understanding.

TOOL 4
STRATEGY SORT

Review a range of solutions based on their potential impact versus the effort required

Strategy Sort is a decision-making tool that helps teams cut through idea overload and decide which solutions are realistically worth pursuing. It allows team members to weigh each option's potential impact against the effort required, so everyone can agree on where to focus first. Strategy Sort will help your team to surface what is effective, feasible and actionable within your current context.

Use this tool to:

- foster discussion and debate about similarities and differences in the teaching practices advocated across a team
- develop a shared understanding of the evidence-informed teaching practices that could be used to improve student learning
- come to a shared understanding of the teaching strategies that your team believes can have the greatest impact on student learning
- explore which of these strategies might be easiest to implement
- agree on the teaching strategies that should be prioritised
- support discussion about enablers or barriers to implementation.

Strategy Sort

What specific outcome or challenge are we focused on improving?

Lower implementation effort

Higher expected impact

Lower expected impact

Higher implementation effort

The solution-finding tool

Sometimes the biggest challenge in school improvement isn't a lack of ideas: it's having too many. Strategy Sort helps teams cut through the noise, weigh their options, and get moving with clarity and confidence.

I once worked with a team that had decided to focus on improving formative assessment. They were full of enthusiasm and had a dozen ideas flying around the room. They were energised but also overwhelmed. They knew they needed to make some choices, but weren't sure how to weigh what was worth pursuing and what to set aside.

So we used Strategy Sort. We mapped each idea using two simple questions: How big is the likely impact? And how hard will it be to implement well? Within 20 minutes, we had surfaced three high-impact, low-effort strategies to start with and secured agreement across the group. They chose to focus on picking non-volunteer routines, mini whiteboards, and exit tickets. The energy in the room shifted. They could finally see a realistic path forward. Strategy Sort helped them get unstuck and find a manageable starting point for action.

That's what this tool offers. A moment to pause, assess and decide. It encourages disciplined professional debate and draws out the collective wisdom in the room. As educators, we often jump into doing without checking whether we're doing the right things, in the right order, at the right time. Strategy Sort slows that impulse just long enough to focus our efforts where they matter most.

It also gives you a record. You'll end the session with a visual map of where your ideas landed: what's in, what's out, and what might be worth returning to later. That means greater alignment and more confidence about what comes next.

This tool is adapted from the classic Impact vs Effort Matrix, a common decision-making framework used across many sectors. Strategy Sort reshapes this model to help education teams collectively assess which teaching strategies are most likely to make an impact and are feasible to implement.

Strategy Sort facilitator guidance

Preparation

This tool works best when you have already identified a specific learning challenge that would benefit from a fresh approach.

You'll need a space suitable for group work. Use an enlarged template or mark up a whiteboard or some butcher's paper with the four descriptions on the template. Label the top centre 'Higher expected impact' and the bottom centre 'Lower expected impact'. Label the left centre 'Higher implementation effort' and the right centre 'Lower implementation effort'.

By the end of the session, the top-right quadrant should clearly highlight the most promising approaches – those that offer significant impact with manageable effort – as priorities to address the identified challenge. Strategies in the top-left quadrant, with high expected impact but considerable implementation effort, also deserve attention. However, the team will need to carefully consider their capacity and available resources to sustainably implement these more demanding shifts in practice.

Step 1: Outline the specific outcomes or challenge area

At the top of the template answer the scoping question: What specific outcome or challenge are we focused on improving?

In some cases this may involve identifying the student learning outcome area (and specific student group, if relevant) that you are focusing on. At other times it might be framed as a teaching and learning problem that we are trying to solve. The group should aim to focus their collective efforts on this specific challenge.

Step 2: Surface a range of strategies

Provide each person with three to five sticky notes or cards and ask them to place them in a line in front of them.

Give each person the following prompt:

'Write down three to five specific teaching strategies that you would recommend teachers use to better enable student learning progress in this outcome area.'

Write one strategy or approach per sticky note in clear, large writing. Ask team members to record each idea on a separate sticky note.

Research upgrade

When in doubt, add research! Where possible, it will be useful for your team to have an opportunity to draw their strategies from relevant research-informed sources, as well as from their own experience. After engaging with some research-informed resources, the group will be able to identify a broader range of potential strategies that could be trialled in the classroom to solve the identified challenge, so aim to prepare some materials for the session if you can. For example, the team could review an applied summary of Rosenshine's Principles of Instruction (Sherrington, 2019), then identify specific strategies that would help them address the challenge of engaging every student actively in class discussions.

Step 3: Sort and debate on the expected impact

In this step, each member of the team places their strategies on the Strategy Sort template. Here, they'll use a relative rating of higher or lower expected impact. They'll explain their thinking, and the team will help to sort the ideas.

- **'Higher expected impact':** These are the teaching practices or strategies that are most likely to have a positive impact on student learning in the chosen focus area.
- **'Lower expected impact':** These are the teaching practices or strategies that are useful, but perhaps relatively less impactful on student learning in this focus area.

Ask one member of the group to place one of their sticky notes on the template and to explain what the strategy is and why they are suggesting the placement they have chosen. Ask if anybody else has a strategy that is similar to this one (even though different words may have been used). Form a cluster of similar sticky notes. It is important that each person explains what each strategy is and why they have placed it in that category. Try to condense the cluster and write it as one fresh sticky note that represents the key shared idea.

Now ask for a second volunteer to share a different sticky note and stick it up. Allow others to add any similar sticky notes to create a cluster. Keep moving through these cycles until there are no more sticky notes remaining across the group.

Throughout the process, discussion and probing questions should be asked.

Here are some useful prompts:

- 'Has this strategy worked for similar learners in the past?'
- 'Have you had personal experience with this approach?'
- 'Could you share a little more about what that strategy would actually look like in practice?'
- 'Do we know if this strategy is supported by any specific research evidence?'

The aim is to gain group consensus on the relative placement of the suggested strategies for expected impact.

Each person in the group has an opportunity to move one of the sticky notes (or an entire cluster of sticky notes if they haven't been condensed into one) and provide their rationale for why it should be placed higher or lower on the expected impact axis. The team can then discuss whether they agree or not. If consensus is not reached, then they can vote. If the majority agrees, it can be moved. Keep the comments and discussion focused and refer to appropriate research or specific experiences wherever possible to justify shifting the strategies.

The goal should be to reduce the number of strategies that are determined to be 'Higher expected impact' down to an essential few. You may also find that some of the strategies are voted off the sheet entirely, as they are not perceived to be worth pursuing.

Step 4: Now for the implementation effort

As we all know, strategies are all well and good until the rubber hits the road on how feasible something is to actually implement. Now it's time to spread out the strategies in the 'Higher expected impact' range to the left or the right. Shift to the left the strategies that the group believes would require 'Higher implementation effort' and shift to the right those that the group rates as requiring 'Lower implementation effort'.

The goal of this additional step is to explore which of the higher-impact strategies are likely to be simple and reliable to implement in practice. Discussion might involve:

- Availability of resources
- Current capability levels
- Alignment with existing practices and routines
- Experience in using such strategies
- Suitability for current environment
- Level of preparation required
- Attention required to successfully deliver
- Availability or reliability of enabling technologies.

Again, work toward gaining group consensus. Given differing experience, expertise and resources in the group, there may be important differences in the ratings that individual group members suggest.

Step 5: Decide on which strategies to try out

Review your completed Strategy Sort and consider the relative impact to effort position of each of the strategies discussed. You may find it helpful to write up these four categories of strategies to define the quadrants:

- **Top right: quick wins** – easy to do, high impact: great early moves to prioritise.
- **Top left: big bets** – high payoff, but require significant investment. We will need to choose wisely and not do too many at the same time.
- **Bottom left: hard slogs** – lots of effort, little return: often best avoided or rethought.
- **Bottom right: nice-to-haves** – low lift required, but not especially valuable. Best to see these as low-priority strategies to return to only after we've secured most of the quick wins and essential big bets.

You are now ready to decide on the strategies that the team feels that they would like to try out. At times, multiple strategies may be chosen and then combined or sequenced as a way of making progress on the challenge you're solving.

> **Top tip!**
>
> Keep a record of your Strategy Sort template and decision-making! While you might choose one or two high-leverage strategies to trial now, you may choose to implement others in the future.

Extension – cross-team challenge

If multiple teams complete the Strategy Sort activity in the same space, you can engage in another round of challenge and feedback. Each team should leave one person behind with their posters or templates as a 'spokesperson'. All other team members should spread out across the other groups. The spokesperson describes the group's current answer to the 'visitors' from other teams. The visitors then have a chance to make comments and leave feedback on sticky notes:

- **Agree** – what do they agree with?
- **Add** – what strategies might the group have overlooked?
- **Challenge** – what do they not agree with?

All educators then return to their original work and revise their answer, incorporating the feedback and insights they have gleaned from other group members.

Strategy Sort example 1 – Choosing formative assessment strategies

School type	Group	How many people	Length of meeting
Secondary	Faculty teams working in a full staff setting	4–7 per team	30–45 mins

Following several whole-school professional learning sessions focused on formative assessment and feedback, the leadership team at a secondary school wanted to help staff move from shared understanding into deliberate action. While staff were positive about the research-informed strategies introduced, there were early signs of overload and uncertainty about where to start. They had new knowledge, but had not yet moved into trialling new practices.

To support teachers in selecting strategies worth investing in first, the leadership team used the Strategy Sort tool during a 45-minute twilight session. Each faculty team worked at their own table with a large version of the Strategy Sort matrix printed on A3 paper.

Amina, a respected teacher leader who had been part of the school improvement team, facilitated the session. She had been supporting the school-wide focus on formative assessment over the past two terms and had drawn heavily on the work of Professor Dylan Wiliam (*Embedded Formative Assessment*, 2018) and Tom Sherrington and Oliver Caviglioli (*Teaching WalkThrus*, 2020). These texts had helped the school develop a shared language around checking for understanding and formative assessment strategies. The school had also printed out the WalkThru visual guides for reference during the session.

'You've all been introduced to a range of formative assessment approaches over the past few weeks,' Amina said. 'The purpose of this session is to help your team choose which of those strategies are most worth trialling. This is about doing fewer things, but doing them well.'

She reminded teachers of three prompts they would be using to guide their discussion:

1. 'What's the expected impact of this strategy on student learning?'
2. 'What's the level of effort or complexity involved in using it well?'
3. 'What can we trial and learn from over the next few weeks?'

Each team was given sticky notes and a short summary handout of formative assessment strategies adapted from *Teaching WalkThrus* and *Embedded Formative Assessment* that they had been introduced to during the PD sessions over the last few terms.

To start, each teacher wrote down two or three strategies they believed were worth considering. Amina encouraged a short period of quiet thinking and said, 'Think about what is likely to make the biggest impact on student learning in your classes.'

Next, teams moved into discussion. One teacher suggested using mini whiteboards to get every student responding during questioning. Another was interested in trying whole-class feedback as a way to reduce marking and improve clarity. Amina moved between groups, using prompts to deepen the discussion:

- 'Have you seen this work in your own classroom or someone else's?'
- 'What makes this high effort or low effort?'
- 'Is this something you'd be confident to test next week?'

As teams placed and clustered their sticky notes on the Strategy Sort grid, a few strong patterns emerged.

In the high-impact, low-effort quadrant, many teams placed:

- Cold calling or 'pick non-volunteers'
- Use of mini whiteboards to check responses of all students
- Exit tickets.

In the high-impact, higher-effort quadrant, they placed:

- Whole-class feedback
- Feedback that moves learning forward
- Hinge questions

- Two starts and a wish
- Short retrieval quizzes.

Strategies considered lower impact or too complex for now, such as lengthy peer marking routines or general comments on student work, were placed in the bottom-left quadrant.

To close the session, Amina invited each team to select two high-impact, lower-effort strategies they felt ready to trial. After a round of discussion, the teams decided that it would be really good to start with 'Pick non-volunteers' and 'Check responses of all students with mini whiteboards', as these are actionable, specific and feasible across multiple classroom contexts. They wrote these on a team planning board, which included space to record reflections during their next meeting.

The Strategy Sort process helped to narrow focus and reduce overwhelm. Teachers left with a clearer sense of what to try, what to set aside for now, and how to support one another. As one teacher said on their way out, 'That was useful. I stopped overthinking it and now I know exactly what I want to take back into the classroom.'

The faculty teams then used a *Teaching Sprints* (Breakspear & Jones, 2020) process to move from identifying the practice into a two to four-week period of intentional, deliberate practice.

Strategy Sort example 2 – Enhancing teaching practice in mathematics

School type	Group	How many people	Length of meeting
Upper primary/ lower secondary	Year 7–9 mathematics teachers	8	30 mins

At a large secondary school, the Year 7–9 mathematics team had spent several weeks reviewing common learning challenges faced by students transitioning from primary. These included difficulty with problem-solving and weak retention of prior learning. To address these issues, the team wanted to focus their teaching energy on a small number of high-impact strategies that could be consistently used across classrooms.

Diego, head of mathematics, and Zara, an early career teacher and member of the school's improvement team, co-facilitated the session. They used the Strategy Sort tool to support the team in making deliberate choices about where to begin.

The team had already spent a number of sessions engaging with background evidence on effective mathematics teaching in lower secondary (Education Endowment Foundation, 2022). Diego said, 'This is our moment to collectively focus – not to do everything at once, but to choose what's most worth focusing on in our practice improvement now.'

He divided the team into pairs, and each pair received a large Strategy Sort matrix with two axes: 'Impact on student learning' and 'Effort to implement well'. Diego distributed sticky notes and a one-page handout summarising eight evidence-informed strategies, including:

- Worked examples with fading
- Diagnostic multiple-choice questions
- Visual models (for example, number lines, bar models)
- Sentence frames for mathematical explanations
- Regular retrieval practice
- Structured pair talk with prompts

- Teaching general problem-solving strategies
- Whole-class feedback.

To begin, each teacher reviewed the strategies and rated them for expected impact. Zara encouraged the group to focus specifically on Years 7 to 9: 'Which of these will help students most?'

Teachers used sticky notes to map out their ratings for relative impact. Then the paired responses were brought together and discussed as a full team. The group noted that worked examples with fading, diagnostic questions, and daily retrieval consistently rated highest across the pairs. These had been highlighted in the research as particularly effective for supporting early secondary students with both fluency and reasoning.

Next, the team rated the strategies by effort or complexity.
Diego asked:

- 'Which of these could we start next week with minimal preparation?'
- 'Which might take more modelling, scaffolding, or planning time?'

Zara shared an insight: 'I've been using diagnostic questions at the start of lessons. It takes a bit of prep, but the quality of discussion that follows has been worth it.' Others agreed, placing it in the high-impact, low-effort quadrant.

By the end of the session, the matrix had taken shape, and the team identified some quick wins and big bets to consider for practice improvement:

- Quick wins – high impact, low effort:
    - Simple diagnostic multiple-choice questions
    - Regular retrieval warm-ups (3–5 minutes)
    - Sentence frames for justifying answers.
- Big bets – high-impact, higher-effort:
    - Worked examples with fading
    - Explicit teaching of general problem-solving strategies
    - Visual models to structure thinking.

To close, Diego invited each teacher to choose one strategy to focus on for the next planning cycle. A few examples included:

- Regular retrieval warm-ups to begin every Year 8 lesson
- Worked examples with fading, for use in an upcoming Year 9 algebra unit.

The team agreed to use a teaching sprints process to trial and reflect on their selected strategies over the following four weeks, with a short check-in scheduled at the end of the term. As the session wrapped up, one teacher said, 'I feel much calmer now. I've felt swamped with ideas lately – this discussion helped me focus on what I can actually work on in my practice this term to make an impact for my students.'

TOOL 5
EVEN BETTER IF

Gain fast, helpful peer feedback to improve the quality of your work

Even Better If is a quick, structured feedback routine that helps your team make good work even better. The Even Better If tool helps teams reflect on what already looks strong – and then stretch toward further incremental improvement. By starting from a strength and asking how it could be enhanced, this approach keeps the tone constructive, avoids blame and invites focused thinking on practical refinements. It's especially useful when draft work is progressing well but there's still room to lift the quality or impact.

Use this tool to:

- collectively improve plans, materials, assessments and resources
- bring in fresh perspectives in a safe and structured setting
- refine and enhance communication pieces (important emails, letters, slides)
- surface ideas and 'wonderings' early in a process
- build a culture of giving and receiving peer feedback.

Even Better If

What specific process, piece of work or practice are we trying to improve?

What's looking strong so far?
Focus on strengths, clarity, and what's likely to have a positive impact.

Even better if
Focus on suggestions and tweaks that could make the work clearer, stronger, or more impactful.

Questions to consider
Raise questions, observations or uncertainties that could help the team clarify, test or strengthen the work.

The refining and enhancing tool

The Even Better If framing is widely used to support actionable peer feedback in education, offering a way to stay constructive and forward-focused. This tool is one of the simplest and most powerful ways to gather helpful feedback on something you're working on. It helps teams move beyond simply thanking and praising colleagues for their efforts, and into a true mindset of improvement. It's a great way to crowdsource practical, thoughtful suggestions, and I find it especially valuable when someone has something that's nearly there but just needs a fresh set of eyes. At times, this tool simply comes down to asking, 'How could we make this 10 per cent better?'

Sometimes we're simply too close to our own work to see what needs refining. Even Better If gives us a safe, structured way to hear others' perspectives – quickly, and without it feeling personal or overwhelming. Whether you're designing a unit, an assessment task, a letter to parents, a new approach to parent–teacher meetings, or a full-day professional learning session, this tool makes it easy to surface helpful thinking from others.

I remember a teacher who had designed a detailed excursion plan. The goal was to make it meaningful and link it to the learning that took place in class. She'd been staring at her screen, stuck in tweak mode. We ran Even Better If, and in 10 minutes, her team offered specific suggestions: 'What will students do during downtime?' 'Is there enough scaffolding to help them make the most of the applied learning tasks?' 'Could we prep them better beforehand to build necessary background knowledge and fluency?' She didn't feel criticised: she felt backed. Those contributions helped her close out the plan, and the trip ultimately became a standout of the term.

Another time, I worked with a deputy principal preparing a full-day professional learning session for the first day back. He was caught in the trap of building more slides, but was stuck on how to make the day more collaborative and engaging. After a quick Even Better If session with his team, a stream of practical, creative ideas emerged: 'What if this section of the day became a structured group task?' 'Could we include a panel with lead practitioners sharing examples so that staff know what this will look like in practice?' 'Let's build in time for team action planning at the end so we all set some clear implementation intentions before getting back to the craziness of our other work.' 'Would you mind if I run a quick energiser after lunch to ensure people are reset and focused for that afternoon session?' The tone was collaborative, focused and energising, and the session was significantly stronger because of it.

What I love about this tool is that it builds a culture of trust and professional generosity. When Even Better If becomes a shared phrase and routine, it creates space to make good work better, faster. It helps teams avoid the trap of holding back useful feedback out of politeness or fear of offending. Over time, it fosters the habits of openness, shared responsibility, and continuous collective improvement. Remember often this is just about helping make good work 10 per cent better.

Even Better If facilitator guidance

Preparation

The Even Better If tool is designed to improve work through collective input. Potential examples include a unit of work, an assessment task, a project-based learning task, a design for a professional learning session, a set of resources and materials, a structure for parent–teacher engagements or a structure for student-led conferences.

The tool can also be used to reflect on a recent implementation experience in order to retrospectively consider how to improve it for next time.

A presenter needs to be allocated to share the work and frame the discussion. In some cases, this presenter might like to send some materials to the team to read beforehand for context.

A shared large copy or wall poster version of the Even Better If template should be used. If using this format, group members can capture their individual thinking on sticky notes before adding them to the shared template. If working remotely, a shared live document, spreadsheet or digital kanban board can be used.

Step 1: Outline the work

Relevant members of the group briefly describe what they are working on and what they are looking for real feedback about.

Remind the group that our intentions are not to be critical but to collectively improve the work, provide fresh insights and offer specific and useful recommendations. Encourage the group to avoid criticism or generalised judgments. Rather, aim for specific, descriptive feedback and actionable recommendations or questions that can improve the work.

Step 2: Gather inputs

Set a timer for 10–15 minutes and have the group review the work (or reflect on their previous experiences of the activity) and add their thoughts as separate comments in the three columns of the template.

It will often work best to provide 3–5 minutes per column and prompt team members to focus only on that column during that allocated block of time. You can use some of the prompt questions to focus the responses.

- **Column 1 – What's looking strong so far?**
  Focus the reflections and comments on strengths, clarity and what's likely to have a positive impact. You can use some additional question prompts such as:
  - What's clear, purposeful or well-considered?
  - Which parts are ready to go as is?
  - What's heading in the right direction?
- **Column 2 – Even better if**
  Encourage the group to focus on manageable suggestions and tweaks that could make the work clearer, stronger or more impactful. Prompt the group further using stems such as:
  - What small changes could strengthen this work?
  - What could be removed to make it clearer?
  - How might this be refined to more fully meet its purpose?
  - How can we make this at least 10 per cent better?

- **Column 3 – Questions to consider**
  This is the space to help the group raise wonderings, questions, observations or uncertainties that could help the team clarify, test or strengthen the work. Help them to surface and capture these unspoken thoughts:
    - What are you still wondering about after reviewing this?
    - What might need more explanation, detail or clarity?
    - What questions would you ask before sharing or using this in practice?

Silent, individual writing and reflection are crucial here. Keep the focus on generating useful notes in each of the columns in the short period of time allocated, rather than drifting into a discussion.

During this step, it can help if the subject whose work is being analysed turns around, or even leaves the group for a period of time. This can help the rest of the team focus on providing thoughtful feedback, rather than getting caught up in a premature discussion with the subject.

Step 3: Discuss and identify emerging themes

Acknowledge the positives that have emerged in the 'What's looking strong so far?' column. Draw out some recurring elements.

Review the team's specific recommendations in the 'Even better if' column. Team members should provide some background on the reasoning behind their responses.

During this period, the presenter should just listen and be open to suggestions without feeling any need to respond, defend or provide further background information. They are welcome to ask clarifying questions.

Step 4: Work through the questions

Take a moment for the presenter to clarify any of the questions that have been listed in the 'Questions to consider' column. Now is not necessarily the time to answer all of them, but you should ensure that there is a clear understanding of what the question is asking, and the background experiences or thinking that have led to it being tabled.

Step 5: Wrap it up

Thank those who have shared and those who have contributed.

Those responsible for the work (if not the entire team) can use the following prompts to identify and review the feedback and make any adjustments to the work plan:

- Where do we feel affirmed?
- What suggestions or ideas resonated with us most – and why?
- What adjustments might we make in light of these responses?
- How have we been encouraged to look at things in a fresh way?
- What specific action steps should we take next?
- Who will take responsibility to move things forward?

The authors of the work don't need to do this live in the presence of the group. Rather, it is often best to simply say thank you and then take time to process and decide what's feasible to refine within the timeline they are working to.

Even Better If example 1 – Strengthening a unit of work

School type	Group	How many people	Length of meeting
Secondary	Science department	9	25 mins

With Week 7 approaching and Term 3 units due for finalisation, each teacher had been working on a unit draft they were responsible for delivering. Angela, the head of science, had been working systematically to move the department away from isolated planning and toward a stronger culture of feedback and shared thinking. She wanted more teachers to actively contribute to the intellectual preparation required to design high-quality units and teach them effectively.

To support this shift, Angela scheduled a focused 25-minute session to help the team sharpen each other's unit plans using a clear and structured process. Ahead of time, she had asked Belinda if she would be happy to go first and bring her draft Year 9 unit on energy. Angela emailed the unit to all staff a few days in advance and printed a few hard copies for the meeting. She also prepared several large A3 versions of the Even Better If tool and placed them on tables, ready for use in trios. Each table had sticky notes and pens available.

When the team arrived, Angela welcomed them and introduced the Even Better If tool as a practical way to strengthen and refine units before they reached the classroom. She explained the three columns they would be working with: 'What's looking strong so far?', 'Even better if' and 'Questions to consider'.

Belinda provided a brief, one-minute overview of the unit's focus and the aspects she was still unsure about. Then the trios got to work, reading through the unit summary and capturing their thinking in each column using the Post-its.

After 10 minutes, each trio shared one insight about what was looking strong so far. A few points of strength were discussed:

- The learning intentions were well-sequenced and included a clear breakdown of concepts into smaller, manageable steps.

This trio explained that this structure helped reduce the likelihood of cognitive overload and supported a smoother progression through the unit.

- The pre-written formative assessments were thoughtfully placed and included multiple-choice hinge questions that could be used to check for understanding before moving on. Teachers noted that these would make it easier to be responsive in their instruction.
- The vocabulary section included guidance on when to pause and build key academic language. Eight essential terms had been broken down using morphology and etymology, helping students develop a deeper conceptual grasp and stronger retention.

In the 'Even better if' column, teachers suggested building in more retrieval practice to help students consolidate their understanding of key energy concepts. One trio proposed adding a short diagnostic task at the start of the unit to check for misconceptions about energy transfer. Another raised the idea of using real-world examples earlier in the sequence to boost engagement and help students connect new content with their own experience.

In the final column, 'Questions to consider', a few logistical and pedagogical points were raised. Would all students be ready to engage with the level of abstract content by Week 3? Had enough time been allowed for practical work and write-ups? Was there a clear plan for extending students who grasped the core concepts early?

Angela captured the key insights and invited Belinda to reflect on what had been most helpful. Belinda noted that having others read the unit with fresh eyes gave her clarity on a few areas she had been unsure about and introduced some practical ideas she hadn't yet considered.

As the timer hit 25 minutes, Angela thanked everyone for offering constructive input and Belinda for being brave and modelling how to seek feedback. 'That was a good use of time,' one teacher said. Angela asked who would be open to sharing their unit and working through a similar process during the next team meeting. Two teachers offered, so Angela suggested they run two 25-minute rounds with a short break in between. That way, they could fit both into the 60-minute meeting.

Belinda followed up with a short email a few days later, sharing the updated unit based on the review. The team agreed to repeat the process for other units as part of the new standard refinement process going forward. A new rhythm of shared ownership and instructional improvement was beginning to take hold.

Even Better If example 2 – Elevating camp planning

School type	Group	How many people	Length of meeting
Lower secondary	Year 7 teachers leading on camp	10	20 mins

With the Term 1 Year 7 camp just a few weeks away, Claire, the Year 7 coordinator, gathered the staff team to review the draft plan. It was mostly finalised, but Claire wanted to create space for feedback before the details were locked in. She introduced the Even Better If tool as a quick, structured way to strengthen what they already had. She had drawn up the three response columns of the tool on a whiteboard: 'What's looking strong so far?', 'Even better if' and 'Questions to consider'.

'This is looking solid,' she said. 'But before we hit go, let's take a moment to ask what could make it even better. Think of it as a final walkthrough, with everyone's eyes on how we can lift the experience for students and staff.'

She gave the team sticky notes and then worked through the three focused prompts on the board. Teachers moved quickly to generate a few individual responses to each prompt. It was clear the team appreciated the opportunity to contribute without it turning into another lengthy planning meeting or having to listen to one or two people dominate the discussion.

After everyone had finished generating sticky notes, Claire invited people to stick their responses for 'What's looking strong so far?' on a shared whiteboard.

A few clear patterns emerged:

- The structure of the daily timetable felt balanced, with a good mix of active and reflective time.
- The staff-to-student ratios were strong, enabling more personalised support and safer supervision.
- The connection to the Term 1 learning goals had been clearly mapped, which gave the camp a strong sense of purpose beyond just fun.

She then moved to asking people to share their responses to 'Even better if'. She gave a prompt: 'I will not take anything you say personally. I honestly just want you to help us make the camp as effective and enjoyable as possible, so please don't hold back any ideas.'

Brett, who didn't usually teach Year 7 but was going to help out on the camp, stuck up his response: 'Let's make sure students wear name tags for at least day one.'

Claire asked him to explain a little more. 'I'll be leading one of the activity groups,' he said, 'but I don't know most of the kids. I don't think all the kids will necessarily know each other either, this early in the year. If I can't use their names, it makes it harder to build trust, especially when managing group dynamics or helping someone settle in.' The group agreed that this simple change could support stronger relationships and facilitate group formation from the outset.

Other ideas followed. Staff suggested adding short orientation activities on the first night to help students settle and connect. Someone raised a concern about long stretches of downtime in the schedule, particularly in the late afternoon when students might become restless. Another asked whether students with higher levels of anxiety had been given enough information ahead of time to prepare themselves mentally for the experience and to understand what would be happening when.

Finally, Claire asked for any Post-its that had been generated in response to 'Questions to consider'. A few logical points emerged regarding who would be travelling on which bus and how students with specific medication needs would be supported throughout the camp.

Claire captured it all and thanked the group for helping her get things right before they were out there with the kids. The staff team was positive about the outcomes of a focused 20-minute Even Better If session. As one teacher said at the end of the session, 'That was great. It felt like we got beyond the logistics and into shaping the human experience we are trying to create.'

Claire embedded the inputs into the materials and sent an email to the team two days later, thanking them for their ideas and sharing the updated resources. The final version of the camp plan was stronger, more considered, and better aligned with what students needed to feel safe, included and ready to engage.

TOOL 6
WE NEED NEXT

Identify professional growth aspirations and actions

We Need Next is a team exercise designed to identify each person's next steps for professional growth. It creates a safe space for everyone to share what support, knowledge or skill they need so the team can help each other and grow together.

Use this tool to:

- identify the potential professional learning needs of the team
- surface the resources and supports that may be available
- match professional learning needs to existing expertise and resources within the team, school or beyond.

We Need Next

Name	1. What specific learning, input or support would help you move forward right now? *(e.g. curriculum guidance, collaborative planning, modelling, co-teaching, observations and feedback, resource recommendations, reading recommendations.)*	2. Who or what could help – within or beyond our team?	3. Next steps to move this forward
1.			
2.			
3.			
4.			
5.			

The professional growth conversation tool

Throughout the busyness of any term, it can be helpful to pause and think deeply about what team members need to continue to grow and develop in their professional practices. Use the We Need Next tool to develop a commitment to ongoing collective improvement and growth, where each member of the team feels safe to share their learning needs and aspirations. It also paves the way for group members to actively support others in their development and growth.

This tool can be particularly useful at the conclusion of a professional learning engagement in order to surface potential next steps in learning. It gives you a structured way to surface people's professional learning gaps, desires and needs across a whole team. I have found it invaluable with teams that have had a number of role changes or reporting-line changes, where things are assumed to be within a certain role's capability but the team member may in fact need upskilling.

We Need Next helps teams surface what they need in order to keep growing before the momentum fades. It's easy to leave a team meeting or professional learning session feeling inspired but unsure what to do next, or where to get support. We Need Next gives everyone a chance to pause, reflect and articulate what would help them most – whether it's a resource, a model, a demonstration, a specific training opportunity or some feedback on practice.

When used regularly, We Need Next helps teams take ownership of their development – and reminds us that we grow best when we grow together. I've seen this tool create powerful 'requests' – for example: 'I'd appreciate it if someone could come into my classroom and tell me honestly how I'm going with this.' 'I'd love to see someone else teach this concept; I just need a clearer picture of how it could look in practice.' 'Has anyone read anything on this that would help me understand it more deeply?'

We Need Next also opens up generous professional 'offers': 'I can help with that.' 'We've got a resource you can borrow.' 'Let's set up a time to work through it.' 'I went to a course on this last year – I'd be happy to share my notes and key insights.'

This tool invites professional vulnerability in a safe, structured way. And it reinforces the idea that growth isn't just about pushing harder; it's about getting the right support, at the right time, from the people around you.

We Need Next facilitator guidance

Preparation

A shared large copy or wall poster version of the We Need Next template should be used. If using this format, group members can capture their individual thinking on sticky notes before adding them to the shared template. If working remotely, a shared live document, spreadsheet or digital brainstorming board can be used. If you have a team greater than five people, use additional copies of the template.

Step 1: Identify the professional learning needs or aspirations

The template prompts the group with this question: What specific learning, input or support would help you move forward right now? One at a time, ask each educator to articulate what they need next in order to further enhance their own teaching knowledge, skills or confidence. Potential requests might include, but are not limited to:

- **Curriculum and content knowledge** – Help me to better understand a certain area of the curriculum or learning progression.
- **Collaborative planning and design** – Provide some additional support with co-planning and instructional sequencing.
- **Modelling and demonstration** – Model the teaching of a specific strategy or technique.
- **In-class guidance and co-teaching** – Co-teach a section of the design with me in my class so that I can build greater confidence in application.
- **Observation and feedback** – Come and observe me teaching and provide some feedback so that I can be sure I am implementing the 'key ingredients' of a strategy effectively.

- **Resources recommendations** – Provide guidance on additional research-based resources that could build out my understanding of the knowledge base.
- **Reading recommendations** – Give suggestions of what else I could read, watch or listen to in order to deepen my understanding.
- **Any other request that can support professional growth and development.**

Record responses in the first column of the template. After doing so, glance through the list and consider the common needs, asks or aspirations across the group to draw out any similarities.

> **Top tip!**
>
> Being willing to be *vulnerable* about potential areas for personal practice development, and being *generous* about sharing what you know with others, are crucial mindsets for this tool to work.
>
> Identifying and meeting needs in a timely way supports the motivation of the team and sustains momentum for ongoing collective professional growth.

Step 2: Surface the supports

The second column of the template prompts the group to consider: Who or what could help – within or beyond our team?

Depending on the needs listed, identify relevant expertise and supports that may be available within the team, school or broader network:

- **Internal team match** – Who has done this before or something similar? Does anyone in the group have particular expertise that we can draw on? Does anyone have a resource that they could share?

- **Across the school match** – Who else across the school has the expertise that could provide us with the needed support? Are there resources or materials that we could try to draw on?
- **Beyond the school** – Who else could we draw on for support and external expertise?

Write the potential matches to each need in the middle column of the template.

For example:

- A team member with expertise in a specific area who could offer to be involved in peer observations
- Drawing on an instructional coach who works within the school to provide some demonstration lessons in order to build confidence in an identified area
- Providing physical resources (such as teaching materials, assessment tasks, manipulatives)
- An offer to provide a live demonstration or video-recorded exemplar lesson segments
- Sharing of links or hard copies of research-informed books, articles, podcasts or videos
- Timetabling for co-planning, co-teaching or peer coaching.

Step 3: Determine actions

Now's the time to allocate the right team members to take action in order to provide the support or resources needed. Try to identify people with well-matched skills, knowledge or resources for each action. The template prompts the team to commit by listing the 'Next steps to move this forward.'

Each team member highlights one action they will take to access the support that they or the team needs, and commits to making it happen by a specific date. Record these on the template for future accountability.

We Need Next example 1 – Using Rosenshine's Principles

School type	Group	How many people	Length of meeting
Secondary	All teacher teams across a staff	60	30 mins

Following a recent series of professional learning sessions on Rosenshine's Principles of Instruction, Rhys, the director of professional learning, wanted to create space for teachers in teams to translate key ideas into personal action for professional growth. During the whole-staff PL, they had read sections of *Rosenshine's Principles in Action* by Tom Sherrington (2019) and watched some video recordings of example lessons. This had created some fresh energy to consider changes in evidence-informed practice. However, Rhys had noticed a pattern emerging from other full-school knowledge-building initiatives: teachers often left inspired but uncertain about where to start or how to maintain the momentum.

To bridge the gap between insight and practice, he scheduled a 30-minute session where each individual team would run the We Need Next tool at a table, but do so live in the room alongside the other teams in the school hall. Rhys introduced it as a way to help teachers name what would support their next steps, and to see how the group might help one another to make progress. 'We've just explored a lot of powerful evidence-informed ideas,' he said. 'Let's take a moment to figure out what each of us needs in order to move forward, and where we can support one another to get started.'

Rhys had prepared a large shared version of the tool on butcher's paper with three columns for each teacher team:

- What support do you need to move forward?
- Who or what could help?
- What's one step you'll take this week?

He handed out sticky notes and invited everyone to reflect quietly and write down one or two things they needed next. 'Think about what would help you feel more confident and ready to apply one of these principles in your teaching.'

After five minutes of silent writing, Rhys asked teachers to place their responses in the first column on their team paper. He then encouraged the team leaders to facilitate the conversation at table groups.

A few patterns began to emerge across the groups:

- Support with co-planning lessons to effectively integrate regular retrieval practice
- Opportunities to observe how others were using questioning techniques to check for understanding
- Adaptable resources or slide decks to support regular review
- Models of scaffolding and gradual release across a lesson sequence
- Access to research-based resources or short readings to deepen understanding of the cognitive science behind the strategies.

Rhys then directed attention to the second column. 'Let's take a few minutes to see who in this room might already have something useful to share,' he said. During one of the table conversations, one teacher offered to demonstrate her whiteboard routines and retrieval prompts. Another volunteered to have two colleagues observe a guided practice lesson. A third had created a bank of exit ticket questions and offered to share the file on the school drive.

To finish the session, Rhys asked everyone to write a small action in the third column. 'It doesn't have to be perfect or polished,' he said. 'Just one step you'll take this week to move your thinking into action.'

Most teachers posted a comment. Rhys then asked team leaders to take a photo of each of the summary sheets and send them to him. He thanked those who had made offers and acknowledged the willingness of each team to be open and practical. He committed to helping shape the school's professional learning agenda around some of the column themes and to working with team leaders to ensure each team had time to follow through on their action commitments.

We Need Next example 2 – Curriculum change

School type	Group	How many people	Length of meeting
Primary	Teacher team	5	15 mins

Amelia, a team leader at a primary school, had already facilitated several professional learning sessions to introduce her team to the new English curriculum. While the group had responded positively, Amelia sensed that enthusiasm was not yet translating into confident planning. Some team members still seemed hesitant, and there were quiet signs of uncertainty about what practical implementation would look like.

Drawing on her experience, Amelia decided to use the We Need Next tool as a way to surface each teacher's immediate needs and help the team clarify what support would make a meaningful difference to their curriculum implementation efforts. She drew up a large shared version of the We Need Next template on butcher's paper and distributed sticky notes to each person.

She was particularly conscious of the importance of psychological safety when navigating change. She wanted to ensure that team members felt confident in speaking up about their concerns and areas that required help. To help model this, she opened the session by acknowledging her uncertainties about the curriculum change. 'I've found restructuring the literacy block a bit overwhelming,' she said. 'There are so many parts we're being asked to rethink, and I'm still finding it hard to let go of some of the old ways I used to get through a lesson that are no longer aligned with the new curriculum.'

Before they began, Amelia had decided to design the session to allow for individual thinking before the group discussion. When she kicked off, she said: 'Let's start with three minutes of silent reflection. Write down one or two things you feel you need next. It might be a resource, a conversation, a modelled lesson, or something else entirely. Just focus on what would help you plan and teach the new English curriculum more effectively.'

After silent writing, Amelia invited the teachers to place their sticky notes in the first column. Then, using one of her go-to prompts, she asked, 'Would anyone like to speak to what they've written, or add anything based on what you're seeing here?'

One by one, the team began to share:

- I want to better understand the key differences between the old and new curriculum.
- Can I see an effective phonics daily review lesson modelled?
- How should spelling instruction be integrated into our planning?
- What assessment strategies should we use to track student progress in reading?
- How exactly should we structure our literacy blocks across the week?
- When and how do effective reading groups happen?
- What can we do about the decreasing quality of writing demonstrated by many students?

Amelia facilitated the discussion by drawing out quieter voices, paraphrasing ideas back to the group, and capturing key themes on the template. As people spoke, she gently prompted others: 'Does anyone else have something else to add?'

As the second column filled up, Jo, one of the more experienced team members, offered to host a phonics demonstration in her classroom the following week and also record a video so that those who couldn't join live could watch it at their convenience. Another teacher shared a unit structure they had already tested out using the new framework. Amelia offered to compile the group's questions about spelling and send them to the curriculum leader at the regional office for guidance on resources that might be helpful.

Before everyone left, Amelia summarised the shared needs, acknowledged the leadership shown by those who had made offers, and thanked the group for leaning into the work together. She took photos of the team's completed tool and promised to follow up with a brief summary email and review the action steps at their next team meeting the following week.

Within a few days, the team had already made progress. Some teachers observed Jo's phonics lesson and held a short debrief afterwards. Amelia shared curated planning resources, responded to follow-up questions, and secured funding for two team members to attend an external workshop on writing instruction.

The team appreciated Amelia's responsive and practical leadership. Her careful facilitation created space for honesty, clarity and momentum. The tool helped to foster a culture of vulnerability and honesty about what it would take for every team member to continue improving.

TOOL 7
START, STOP, CONTINUE

Work out what we need to do in order to maximise team effectiveness

Start, Stop, Continue is a simple reflection tool that helps your team take stock of how you work and make quick improvements. It asks everyone to pinpoint what to start doing, what to stop doing, and what to continue so you can keep getting better as a team. Too often we continue with the status quo just because it's the way that things have 'always been done'. This tool forces us to critically analyse and self-reflect as a team and intentionally be open-minded to change.

Use this tool to:
- work out if current systems and processes are as effective as they could be
- assess if current programs need to be changed
- stop ineffective teaching practices.

Start Stop Continue

Focus for this review:

Start	Stop	Continue

The tool for taking stock and making simple adjustments

Sometimes the simplest tools are the most powerful. Start, Stop, Continue is your go-to when a team needs to take stock of a program, a routine or a way of working and decide what's actually worth carrying forward. It helps cut through the noise and name what's helping, what's hindering and what needs to evolve. It's also a great way to create space for improvement, without getting stuck in blame or endless debate.

Schools can easily fall into a kind of professional groundhog day, rolling through the same meetings, processes and routines week after week, term after term; often repeating things that aren't working or are creating pent-up frustration. This tool breaks that cycle. Its clear categories help everyone generate ideas quickly based on lived experience. The 'Stop' column, in particular, is powerful – it gives teams permission to let go of things that no longer serve their purpose or are delivering diminishing returns.

I remember using this tool with a team that was reflecting on how they were running their weekly meetings. Everyone was exhausted, and the meetings had started to feel like a box-ticking exercise. When we asked, 'What's one thing we should stop doing?' the answers came fast: 'reading updates off slides'; 'long debriefs that turn into monologues'. What should we start doing? 'Tighter agendas', 'rotating facilitators', 'actually using a protocol to structure the thinking'. And what should we continue? 'Celebrating quick wins', 'keeping the first five minutes for connection', 'having data as the basis of our discussion'. That 20-minute conversation tool reset their whole approach and avoided another term of building frustration and decreasing engagement.

What I love about this tool is that it reinforces a simple idea: we can keep getting better, as long as we take a moment to reflect. Used regularly, Start, Stop, Continue builds a culture of practical, incremental improvement, where agency, not inertia, shapes how we work together.

I've seen and used many different versions of this classic tool. You should feel free to use the version that works best for you and your team.

Start – Stop – Continue
- *Start* – What should we begin doing to improve or move forward?
- *Stop* – What's not working or no longer serving its purpose?
- *Continue* – What's working well and should be sustained?

Begin – Drop – Sustain
- *Begin* – What should we introduce or try that we're not currently doing?
- *Drop* – What's no longer serving its purpose and needs to be let go?
- *Sustain* – What's working well and should be maintained as is?

Do more – Do less – Keep doing
- *Do more* – What deserves more attention, energy or emphasis?
- *Do less* – What's taking too much time or not adding enough value?
- *Keep doing* – What's working well and should stay as part of our regular practice?

Launch – Let go – Lock in
- *Launch* – What should we start or trial that could help us improve?
- *Let go* – What's slowing us down or taking us off course?
- *Lock in* – What's worth embedding and committing to over time?

Keep – Polish – Cut
- *Keep* – What's working well and doesn't need to change?
- *Polish* – What has potential but needs refining or improving?
- *Cut* – What's not effective and should be removed?

Create – Cherish – Chuck
- *Create* – What should we start doing, build or experiment with?
- *Cherish* – What really matters and should be protected or prioritised?
- *Chuck* – What should we stop doing because it no longer adds value?

Start Stop Continue facilitator guidance

Preparation

The facilitator needs to choose the focus topic prior to the session. This may be based on:

- Outcomes from previous conversation tools
- Wanting to reassess current practices or processes
- Data – or even a hunch – that you have something that could be improved.

The template can be either printed out or replicated onto a board. Participants can capture their thinking on sticky notes before adding them to the template.

Step 1: Orient the team

It is important to introduce the Start, Stop, Continue tool by stating that part of our job as teachers is to continually strive to do what is best for our students. Sometimes that will mean stopping things that have become ingrained in us as teachers. The flipside of this is that it also gives us the exciting opportunity to start something new, or to get even better results from something we've been doing the same way for a long time. You may need to emphasise that a couple of our norms are to 'Make room for new thinking' and 'Invite healthy challenge', given that many of us find changes to how we do things very challenging to consider.

Step 2: Introduce the topic

Provide an overview of what you will be getting the team to reflect on.

If the topic is related to a program or service, you may need to tell the participants what the topic is prior to your meeting. This will give them time to consider potential alternatives.

Step 3: Generate individual ideas

Provide each participant with sticky notes and ask them to individually write down ideas for strategies, actions or approaches that the team could:

1. Start (new practices worth adopting)
2. Stop (current practices that aren't effective or useful), and
3. Continue (current practices that are effective and should remain).

Encourage participants to note down their ideas clearly and succinctly, without worrying about justification or detailed explanation at this stage.

Step 4: Cluster and categorise ideas

Invite participants to place their sticky notes under the headings 'Start', 'Stop' and 'Continue' on a shared template or visible surface. Work collaboratively to cluster similar or overlapping ideas together, making the group's collective thinking visible.

Where participants have differing opinions on categorisation, facilitate open discussion and respectful debate. Allow individuals to share their reasoning and justification, ensuring all voices are heard. Once discussed, try to gain consensus on which ideas fit in each of the three categories.

Step 5: Determine clear next steps

For actions identified in the 'Continue' category, clearly reinforce their significance, highlighting the need for intentional effort to sustain and enhance these effective practices.

Guide the team to prioritise the actions within each category, clearly sequencing them based on urgency, feasibility and potential benefits. Assign specific timeframes for starting new actions or stopping existing ones. Where immediate decisions can't be made, identify clearly defined next steps, such as gathering additional information or assigning further exploration tasks. Confirm explicit roles and responsibilities to ensure accountability and momentum.

Start, Stop, Continue example 1 – Strengthening planning meetings

School type	Group	How many people	Length of meeting
Primary or secondary	Any teacher team	4–7 depending	20 mins

At a local school, a teacher team met at the end of Week 6 in Term 3 to review the progress of their collaborative planning meetings. They had adopted a new fortnightly structure earlier in the term, with fewer meetings but longer blocks of time, and were beginning to experience some early frustrations. A few sessions had drifted off course, and some teachers were unclear about the actions that had been decided by the end of the meetings.

To support a quick reset, Leanne, the team leader, decided to use the Start, Stop, Continue tool – but to mix it up, she used the 'Keep, Polish, Cut' version. She introduced it at the beginning of the session as a focused way to reflect on the team's current habits and make small, intentional adjustments to how they worked together.

'I know we've made some good progress with our planning format this term,' she said. 'But I've noticed we're still not finishing with clear next steps. Rather than let that pattern continue, I thought we could step back and sharpen a few things together.' She framed the session as a chance to reflect honestly without judgment. 'This isn't about fixing everything. Let's focus on simple changes that will help us use this time more effectively in the weeks ahead.'

She had written the three category headings on a large piece of butcher's paper and handed out sticky notes. Then she gave a short prompt: 'We'll begin with two minutes of silent thinking. Aim for at least one idea in each category. Don't overthink – just jot down whatever comes to mind.'

After a few minutes of writing, Leanne invited the team to begin sharing with the 'Keep' column. She employed a structured approach to elicit ideas and foster consensus. 'David, can we start with one of your "Keep" notes?' she asked. David shared his idea: rotating the facilitator role. Leanne added it to the butcher's paper and asked, 'Does anyone else have something similar?' Two others had noted the same idea, using slightly different language. Leanne grouped the sticky notes together and read them aloud.

She then asked, 'Does anyone have a different idea we should consider for this column?' One teacher mentioned the value of using shared planning documents. Another highlighted the five-minute wrap-up they had begun trialling to confirm actions at the end of each session. Leanne added both and asked, 'Do we agree these are things worth protecting?'

By the end of the discussion, the 'Keep' column included:

- Rotating the facilitator role so everyone shares responsibility
- Using shared planning documents to co-design units and sequences
- Setting aside five minutes at the end to confirm next steps and responsibilities.

Next, the group moved to the 'Polish' column. Leanne followed the same process, prompting each teacher to share and cluster similar ideas. The discussion focused on minor but meaningful adjustments to their existing habits. Suggestions in the 'Polish' column included:

- Begin each meeting by stating the main outcome and allocating time to each agenda item
- Use a visible timer to stay on track during longer discussions
- Assign one person to capture discussion points and next steps in a shared document
- Create a short agenda template so meetings can be pre-structured more easily
- Have a 'car park' sheet for questions or ideas that aren't directly related to the session focus.

In the 'Cut' column, they agreed to let go of:

- Trying to cover too many agenda items in a single session

- Long detours into unpacking specific incidents of individual student behaviour
- Keeping laptops open unless being used for shared planning, with a no-email policy
- Spending the first 10 minutes catching up socially before starting
- Discussing non-urgent operational details that could be handled via email.

At one point, a conversation began to drift into a broader issue around team workload. Leanne paused the group and gently redirected using the norm: 'Let's stick to what matters for this session. We're focusing on how we plan together. We can come back to that bigger question another time.' The prompt helped the team refocus and stay within the scope of the conversation.

As the discussion wrapped up, Leanne summarised the key themes and helped the team decide what to trial first. 'Let's start with the visible timer and shared note-taking,' she said. One teacher volunteered to bring in a timer, and another offered to try out the note-taking role and set up a shared document on Microsoft Teams for their next meeting. Leanne took a photo of the completed chart, uploaded it to their shared team folder, and closed the session with a clear next step: 'We'll revisit this at the start of Week 8 and see what's helping and what still needs adjusting.'

By the next meeting, the changes were already noticeable. The session remained focused, next steps were clearly captured, and the group finished on time. They continued to use the same tool once a term to steadily improve the way they structured and ran their collaborative planning block.

Start, Stop, Continue example 2 – Aligning with a system-wide teaching policy

School type	Group	How many people	Length of meeting
Secondary	Full staff	50	45 mins

When the education system released a new policy outlining a clearly defined learning and teaching model, the leadership team at a secondary school recognised the importance of aligning their current instructional practices with the updated expectations. While the school's existing approaches were seen as strong overall, the leadership team also identified gaps and inconsistencies that needed attention.

To open up this conversation with staff, Maya, the director of teaching and learning, designed a 45-minute session using the Start, Stop, Continue tool. She framed the session as a collaborative opportunity to reflect on current practice in light of the policy shift and identify priority adjustments the school could make together.

'This is not about scrapping what we do,' Maya said as the session began. 'It's about sharpening our focus and making sure that what we're doing day to day aligns with what the system is asking of us. Let's use this tool to help us step back and look at the bigger picture together.'

Maya had written the three columns – 'Continue, Stop, Start' – on four sets of butcher's paper placed around the staffroom and provided sticky notes on each table. Given that she wanted to emphasise what could stay the same during this period of policy change, she flipped the order of the typical Start, Stop, Continue tool. To give structure, she prompted everyone with three focused questions:

- 'What should we continue because it's working well and already aligned?'
- 'What should we stop that no longer reflects high-impact practice?'
- 'What should we start doing that better aligns with the new model?'

Maya gave the team five minutes of silent writing time, encouraging each person to contribute at least one sticky note to each column. 'Write down specific, tangible classroom practices. Don't worry about the perfect description – you'll have a chance to flesh it out during discussion.'

After the silent reflection, staff moved around the room in small groups to post their notes. Maya asked each group to focus on one column at a time, starting with 'Continue', so the session began with a clear view of what didn't need to change despite the policy update. Some of the 'Continue' practices that emerged included:

- Clearly stating learning intentions and success criteria
- Regularly using formative assessment strategies to check for understanding
- Establishing consistent lesson routines that support focus and attention
- Encouraging student metacognition and agency in learning.

Next, the groups rotated to the 'Start' column. Maya prompted them to cluster similar ideas and begin reading through each other's notes. As she circulated, she used prompts like, 'Can anyone explain what this would look like in practice?' and 'Which of these would be quick wins we could implement this term?' Staff suggested several clear 'Start' practices:

- Consistently using worked examples to scaffold student practice
- Incorporating regular review or retrieval practice at the start of lessons
- Using visual scaffolds and sentence stems to support all learners
- Providing guided practice and checking for success before expecting extended periods of independent work.

In the 'Stop' column, the team identified several practices that were common but misaligned:

- Relying on volunteer responses rather than using techniques to check all students' thinking

- Allowing extended independent work before students had successfully practised with guidance
- Jumping into multiple content-heavy lessons without checking prior knowledge.

As the ideas settled, Maya brought the group back together to surface key themes that had been captured across the large sheets. 'What are we starting to see as priorities here?' she asked. One teacher noted that many of the 'Start' and 'Stop' items connected to the same big idea: making thinking visible and being responsive. Another pointed out that a few of the 'Continue' strategies could be strengthened with more consistency across classrooms.

To close the session, Maya asked each teacher to identify one actionable insight from the wall and discuss how they could bring it into their teaching the following week. A few teachers volunteered to trial small changes and report back. Others asked for follow-up support and booked in instructional coaching sessions.

The leadership team took photos of the butcher's paper and used the feedback to refine their whole-school instructional model to better align with the new policy. They also began mapping out a term-by-term professional learning sequence based on the patterns that had emerged in the session.

As one teacher reflected in a follow-up conversation, 'It was refreshing to look at policy alongside what we're already doing and come out with a clearer focus on what can stay the same and where we need to focus our change efforts.'

Start, Stop, Continue example 3 – Enhancing full-school PD design

School type	Group	How many people	Length of meeting
All school types	Leadership team	10+ depending on team size	25 mins

A week after a full-day staff professional learning event focused on evidence-informed teaching practices, the senior leadership team invited the team leaders to reflect on the experience using a structured feedback process. The goal was to gather practical insights that could be used to refine future professional learning days and better meet teachers' needs.

Jamal, the assistant principal responsible for professional learning, introduced the reflection session as the first agenda item in the team meeting. He framed it as a quick and constructive way to capture input while the experience was still fresh. 'Last week was a big day of learning for our staff,' he said. 'Today we want to take a few minutes to reflect, not just on content, but on how we structure these days going forward. Our aim is to keep building professional learning that is focused, energising and useful.'

Rather than using the familiar 'Start, Stop, Continue' language, Jamal introduced a variation of the tool called 'Create, Cherish, Chuck'. He explained, 'We want to make space for new ideas, hold on to what really worked, and let go of the things that got in the way. This framing helps us name all three clearly.'

Before beginning the activity, he reminded the team leaders of the three collaboration norms they had been working with throughout the year:

- Stick to what matters
- Make room for new thinking
- Invite healthy challenge.

'These norms will guide our thinking,' Jamal said. 'Let's focus on what really matters, stay open to fresh perspectives, and be willing to say what's not working, even if it's been around for a while.'

He had drawn up the three columns – 'Create, Cherish, Chuck' – on a whiteboard at the front of the room. Sticky notes were on the tables. Jamal gave the following prompts:

- 'What should we create next time to make these days more useful or engaging?'
- 'What should we cherish and carry forward because it really worked?'
- 'What should we chuck because it didn't serve us well?'

He gave team leaders two minutes of silent reflection and writing time after each prompt. 'Try to name specific elements such as timing, delivery, content or structure. Don't hold back – just be honest and constructive.'

After writing, each team leader put their sticky notes up and read what others had posted. Jamal used facilitation prompts to extend the thinking:

- 'Can you give a quick example of how that played out?'
- 'Would this change benefit all staff or specific groups?'
- 'What would this look like if we trialled it next time?'

Several clear patterns began to emerge.

In the 'Create' column, staff suggested:

- Shorter, more interactive workshop blocks
- More time in role-alike groups to explore practical applications
- Teacher-led case studies based on internal expertise
- Built-in planning time to adapt materials for classroom use.

In the 'Cherish' column, team leaders highlighted:

- Clear pre-reading or framing materials shared ahead of time
- Time for collaborative reflection and group debriefs

- Practical classroom strategies from presenters, with ready-to-use resources.

In the 'Chuck' column, team leaders agreed to let go of:

- Long back-to-back sessions with no breaks
- Content-heavy presentations late in the day
- Abstract theory with limited classroom relevance.

Once the sharing was complete, Jamal brought the group back together. He summarised what had surfaced and acknowledged the thoughtfulness of the feedback. 'This is really helpful,' he said. 'I'm hearing a strong desire for more practical time, better pacing, and fewer things crammed in.'

To close the tool discussion, he invited team leaders to flag if they would be open to contributing to a focused working group to progress some of the ideas and ensure they were baked into the next full-staff PD day at the start of the following term.

The senior leadership team photographed the butcher's paper, pulled together a summary of key insights, and used it to shape the design of their next PD day alongside the working group.

In the following PD day, the changes were clear. Sessions were shorter and more interactive. Practical time was built into the agenda. The whole day felt better paced. As one teacher put it, 'That felt like it was built with us in mind, not just delivered to us.'

CONCLUSION
OVER TO YOU

You know the feeling. A calendar invite drops into your inbox entitled 'All team collaborative time'. You wonder whether it will have any value or just be another hour that feels like a bit of a waste. Then, later in your career, you become the one sending that invitation, responsible for structuring the session, often without a clear understanding of how to make it genuinely useful.

Most of us care deeply about using collaborative time well, but we're also stretched, under pressure and often running these sessions without much support. That's why I created this toolkit – to help structure the time we already have and make it count, without needing to build something from scratch every time.

Throughout the book, I've shared field-tested tools and routines that can help you cut through the noise, engage people, and move conversations forward. You don't have to be a natural facilitator or spend hours preparing. The tools are designed to do the heavy lifting for you.

But like any professional practice, one-off use is only part of the picture. The most significant impact comes when you find a rhythm. Use these tools regularly with your team and you'll build momentum and new norms over time.

Collaboration time shapes culture. If team meetings are poorly run, it sends a message that our shared time doesn't matter. But when we plan that time well, we create space for honest thinking, shared decisions and collective progress. That's what elevated conversations are all about.

You don't need to change everything at once. Start with one team, one tool and one session. Try it. Adapt it. Then try again. That's how new habits form and new ways of working begin to take hold.

Once you have a clear understanding of the purpose of each tool and feel confident about how to navigate the core steps, you can move beyond the tool as written and focus more on the interaction itself. You'll soon find your own way to adapt, evolve and make the work your own.

At their best, elevated conversations lead to more than just better meetings. They help build elevated connections between staff, generate deeper collective thinking, and result in stronger, more aligned professional practice. That's the real goal: stronger teams and better outcomes for learners.

You don't need to get it perfect. Just get it moving. One clear, structured conversation can shift the tone of a team. And those shifts, over time, shape the culture of a school.

> Please visit **https://elevatedconversations.com.au** to download resources, gain inspiration and share your insights on how to make the most of the collaborative time we already have.

APPENDIX A
FACILITATOR PLANNING TOOL

Before running any session, it's helpful to spend a few minutes clarifying what you're trying to achieve and how you'll use the tools to guide the conversation. This simple planning template supports you in clarifying the purpose, choosing the right tool, and thinking ahead about how to structure the session. Use it to build confidence, stay focused and avoid overloading your sessions.

Elevated Conversation Session Designer

Team/group: _____ Date: _____ Time block/s: _____

Protocol/s (tick relevant):
1. Empathy Square
2. Deeper Reasons
3. Outcome Heat Map
4. Strategy Sort
5. Even Better If
6. We Need Next
7. Start, Stop, Continue

What do you aim to achieve by using this protocol? What are you hoping to explore with your team?

Session component	What will you do at each stage to support a successful conversation?
1. Set it up • How will I physically set up the space to support the type of interactions we want? • What materials do I need? • What do participants need to see, hear or read in advance? • What template or shared surface will we use to capture group thinking?	
2. Run it • How will I open the session to create energy and focus? • What framing or prompt will connect us to the challenge? • What norms or behaviours will I reinforce during the session? • How will I support balanced participation and draw out all voices? • Where do I anticipate that the conversation may get stuck?	
3. Close in motion • How will we capture and record the group's key thinking? • How will I wrap up with clarity and momentum about next steps? • What tone or message do I want to leave the group with?	

APPENDIX B
FACILITATOR REFLECTION QUESTIONS

After any session, it's worth taking a moment to step back and reflect. This tool helps you review what worked, where the group made progress, and what you might tweak next time. Use it to sharpen your facilitation over time and stay focused on what your team needs most.

1. Purpose and structure:

- Did we stay focused on the core purpose of the session?
- Was the tool well-matched to what the team needed?
- Did the steps flow smoothly, or did I need to adapt in the moment?
- Would I use this tool again for a similar purpose?

2. Group dynamics and engagement:

- Did people stay engaged and contribute meaningfully?
- Did I notice patterns of participation: who spoke, who didn't, who dominated?
- Were the collaboration norms visible in how the group worked together?
- Was there enough room for new thinking and respectful challenge?

3. Facilitation moves:

- What worked in how I guided the session?
- What felt clunky or could be improved next time?
- Did I do enough to capture the group's thinking in a visible, useful way?
- What did I learn about how this team works and what they might need next?

REFERENCES

Boudreau, E. (2019, October 22). *The right way to lead teacher learning.* Harvard Graduate School of Education. https://www.gse.harvard.edu/news/uk/19/10/right-way-lead-teacher-learning

Breakspear, S., & Jones, B. R. (2020). *Teaching sprints: How overloaded educators can keep getting better.* Corwin Press.

Danielson, C. (2012). *Talk about teaching! Leading professional conversations.* Corwin.

Education Endowment Foundation. (2018). *Improving literacy in key stage 2: Guidance report.* https://educationendowmentfoundation.org.uk/education-evidence/guidance-reports/literacy-ks2

Education Endowment Foundation. (2019). *Improving literacy in secondary schools: Guidance report.* https://educationendowmentfoundation.org.uk/education-evidence/guidance-reports/literacy-ks3-ks4

Education Endowment Foundation. (2022). *Improving mathematics in key stages 2 and 3: Guidance report* (2022 update). https://educationendowmentfoundation.org.uk/education-evidence/guidance-reports/maths-ks-2-3

Evidence for Learning. (2020). *Improving mathematics in upper primary and lower secondary.* Evidence for Learning.

Grant, A. (2021). *Think again: The power of knowing what you don't know.* Penguin.

Gray, D., Brown, S., & Macanufo, J. (2010). *Gamestorming: A playbook for innovators, rulebreakers, and changemakers.* O'Reilly Media.

Grinder, M. (1997). *The elusive obvious: The science of nonverbal communication.* Michael Grinder and Associates.

Hochman, J. C., & Wexler, N. (2017). *The writing revolution: A guide to advancing thinking through writing in all subjects and grades.* Jossey-Bass.

Robinson, V. M. J. (2017). *Reduce change to increase improvement.* Corwin Press.

Senge, P. M. (2006). *The fifth discipline: The art and practice of the learning organization* (Revised Ed.). Broadway Business.

Sherrington, T. (2019). *Rosenshine's principles in action.* John Catt.

Sherrington, T., & Caviglioli, O. (2020). *Teaching Walkthrus: Five-step guides to instructional coaching* (Vol. 1). John Catt Educational Ltd.

Wiliam, D. (2018). *Embedded formative assessment* (2nd ed.). Solution Tree Press.

Willingham, D. T. (2017). *The reading mind: A cognitive approach to understanding how the mind reads.* Jossey-Bass.

INDEX

5 Whys 64

active facilitation ix, 15, 27–34
action point 33
adapting the process 43–44
adjustments 30, 51, 83–85, 111, 131, 135–136, 138
agency x, 131, 139
auditing 19–20

big bets 97–104
broader ownership 9

clear purpose 9, 109
close in motion 27–34, 148
collaborative time ix, 4–6, 15, 17–20, 145–146
connection conversation 47–48
culture 17, 3, 105, 108, 131, 145–146

decisions 7, 33, 36, 47, 91–93
decision point 33
Deeper Reasons 7, 22–25, 61–75, 148
dialogue 11, 16, 40
different opinions 33
disagreement 5, 33, 36, 38

documenting 33

elevated conversations 4–7, 9–10, 15, 43–44, 145–146
Empathy Square 7, 22–25, 45–60, 148
essential to learn 24, 78–89
Even Better If 7, 22–26, 105–116, 148
expected impact 92–97, 100, 103

facilitation ix–x, 10–11, 15, 22, 27–34, 43, 149–150
Facilitator Planning Tool 147–148
Facilitator Reflection Questions 149–150
feelings wheel 51
formative assessment strategies 99–100, 139
framing 58, 63–64, 107, 141, 148

group discussion 18, 32, 37, 125
group norms 15, 35–40
group thinking 32, 148

hard slogs 97–104
harder to teach 24, 78–89
higher expected impact 92–97

ideas xi, 4, 8, 30, 35–39, 71–72, 93–95, 115, 123, 134–136
identifying ix, 15, 18–20
impact ix–x, 6–7, 91–106
implementation effort 92, 94–98
important to learn 78–89
improvement xi, 6, 31, 77, 93, 102–103, 107–108, 129–131
inclusive 8–9, 22
individual thinking 32, 37, 48, 64, 108, 120, 125
invite healthy challenge 16, 36–38, 40, 70, 84, 133, 141
learning prioritisation conversation 79–80
lifting 24–25
lower expected impact 92–97

make room for new thinking 16, 36–40, 58, 70, 133, 141,

nice-to-haves 97-104
norms 15–16, 35–40, 145, 148–149

Outcome Heat Map 7, 22–25, 77–89, 148
ownership x, 9, 36, 114, 119

pairs 28–29, 32, 102–103
prepare ix–x, 28, 43
problem-framing conversation 63–64
professional conversations xi, 3, 6
professional growth 7, 22, 117, 119–121, 123
professional learning conversations 3
professional learning needs 117, 120–121

question prompts 33, 109
questions to consider 106–116
quick wins 97–104, 131, 139

reasons 61–75
refining and enhancing tool 107–108
Reflect–Discuss–Share 29
right tool 15, 21–26, 147
run the session 27–30, 34

Say, Do, Think, Feel 49–60
set it up 27–30, 34, 148
simple adjustments 131–132
solution-finding tool 93
start small 20, 44
Start, Stop, Continue 7, 22–25, 28, 129–143, 149
stick to what matters 16, 36–40, 73, 87, 137, 141
Strategy Sort 7, 22–25, 39, 91–104
structured process 9

taking stock 131–132
tangible output x, 9
team effectiveness 129–143
team time x, 15, 17–20
thinking together 11
three-point communication 8–9, 55
time 3–5, 15, 17–20, 31, 44, 145–146
time-bound 9
toolkit 6–7, 9, 41–143
tools xi, 7–9, 21–25, 145

We Need Next 7, 22–25, 117–127, 149
weary talk 5–6, 17
what's looking strong so far? 106–116

www.ingramcontent.com/pod-product-compliance
Lightning Source LLC
Chambersburg PA
CBHW071206070526
44584CB00019B/2938